"With practical information and resources plus candid, personal stories in every chapter, *"Mom, Dad . . . I'm Pregnant"* will help families make sense of their circumstances and move ahead wisely. By the grace of God, families can be restored, and this book will surely help."

—MARGARET HARTSHORN, president, Heartbeat International

"Mom, Dad . . . I'm Pregnant" goes straight to the heart of every parent's worst fear. Jayne Schooler is honest and informative, and powerfully communicates hope when most parents feel despair. A must-read for any person who's on this rocky path."

—CATHERINE HICKEM, LCSW, Kingdom Princess® Ministries

From a much needed perspective, Jayne Schooler proves that love and grace can triumph even when facing an intensely personal and heartbreaking family crisis. I highly recommend this book!

—JOHN ENSOR, president, A Woman's Concern Pregnancy Health Services, Boston

"Forty years ago my parents heard the same stunning announcement from me that Jayne Schooler heard from her daughter. How I wish we would have had such a tool as this. I know it will be a blessing for those who don't know where to turn, what to say and what to do."

—SHERRIE ELDRIDGE, author of *Twenty Things Adopted Kids Wish Their Adoptive Parents Knew* and *Twenty Life-Transforming Choices Adoptees Need to Make*

"Mom, Dad . . . I'm Pregnant" is a wonderful tool for parents facing an unplanned, untimely pregnancy. It is comforting and insightful, confronting difficult issues directly. Schooler gives hope to the reader, reminding them that through all, God is ever present.

—GLENN DE MOTS, president, Bethany Christian Services

"mom,dad

...I'm pregnant

when your daughter or son faces an unplanned pregnancy

Jayne E. Schooler

NAVPRESS®

BRINGING TRUTH TO LIFE

OUR GUARANTEE TO YOU

The Navigators is an international Christian organization. Our mission is to reach, disciple, and equip people to know Christ and to make Him known through successive generations. We envision multitudes of diverse people in the United States and every other nation who have a passionate love for Christ, live a lifestyle of sharing Christ's love, and multiply spiritual laborers among those without Christ.

NavPress is the publishing ministry of The Navigators. NavPress publications help believers learn biblical truth and apply what they learn to their lives and ministries. Our mission is to stimulate spiritual formation among our readers.

© 2004 by Jayne E. Schooler

All rights reserved. No part of this publication may be reproduced in any form without written permission from NavPress, P.O. Box 35001, Colorado Springs, CO 80935.
www.navpress.com
NAVPRESS, BRINGING TRUTH TO LIFE, and the NAVPRESS logo are registered trademarks of NavPress. Absence of ® in connection with marks of NavPress or other parties does not indicate an absence of registration of those marks.
ISBN 1-57683-482-4

Cover design by Brand Navigation, LLC—DeAnna Pierce, Bill Chiaravalle, www.brandnavigation.com
Creative Team: Dan Rich, Traci Mullins, Arvid Wallen, Darla Hightower, Pat Miller

Some of the anecdotal illustrations in this book are true to life and are included with the permission of the persons involved. All other illustrations are composites of real situations, and any resemblance to people living or dead is coincidental.

Unless otherwise identified, all Scripture quotations in this publication are taken from the *New King James Version* (NKJV). Copyright © 1982 by Thomas Nelson, Inc. Used by permission. All rights reserved.

Schooler, Jayne E.
  Mom, dad-- I'm pregnant : when your daughter or son faces an unplanned pregnancy / By Jayne E. Schooler.-- 1st ed.
     p. cm.
  Includes bibliographical references.
  ISBN 1-57683-482-4
  1. Teenage pregnancy. 2. Pregnancy, Unwanted--Psychological aspects.
3. Pregnancy--Religious aspects--Christianity. 4. Parent and adult
child. 5. Abortion--Religious aspects--Christianity. 6.
Parents--Attitudes. I. Title.
   HQ759.4.S35 2004
   306.874--dc22

                                        2004016997

Printed in Canada

1 2 3 4 5 6 7 8 9 10 / 08 07 06 05 04

FOR A FREE CATALOG OF
NAVPRESS BOOKS & BIBLE STUDIES,
CALL 1-800-366-7788 (USA)
OR 1-416-499-4615 (CANADA)

dedication

To Ray, our son and brother,
    thank you for standing in the gap.
To Micah Benjamin and Annalise Elizabeth,
    you bring us unspeakable joy!

contents

part three   MENDING THE FAMILY TAPESTRY

foreword

I JUST LOVE to travel. The thought of a new adventure to unexplored territories excites me. It is great fun to check out the map, read travel guides, and talk to others who have charted those places before me. Once I know where I want to go, I do what I can to experience the journey to the fullest.

For those of you who have picked up this book, you have been on a journey with your son or daughter, or you're about to embark on one. It is a journey none of you had made plans for nor did you want to take this trip. That is the way with life. We have dreams and plans for our future and the future of our children, but more often than not, there are unexpected bumps and turns along the way.

As parents, you spend many hours dreaming about the time when you have completed your work and have launched your child on his or her own journey of independence. At one time your dreams consisted of the day when your child would come to you announcing that he or she is in love and is making plans to marry. Hopefully, in the years that followed, your dreams of becoming a grandparent would be fulfilled. However, for many of you those dreams died with the news from either your son or daughter that a baby was conceived long before those dreams were fulfilled. Without your consent, you are compelled to take a journey without even a map— much less travel guides or others to talk to who have been on that journey.

Your journey reminds me of a wonderful allegory story written by Hannah Hurnard in her book, *Hind's Feet on High Places*. In that story, a young girl named Much Afraid is embarking on a journey with the encouragement of the Great Shepherd to the high places where she will be made whole again. It is a difficult journey filled with valleys, darkness, and rocky crags. The Shepherd gives her two companions to help her along; their names are Pain and Suffering. As a counselor, I have had the privilege of walking that journey with many parents. I have been able to encourage them that there is wholeness ahead. To reach that goal, Pain and Suffering are often their companions. The journey is rough and complicated. But restoration and freedom are ahead.

This book offers you a road map to help you find your way. You do not have to go on this journey alone. Others have shared their stories to give you direction, encouragement, and hope. Within these pages you will receive guidance and direction down three different paths. Each one is filled with shock, anxiety, apprehension, confusion, and heartache. However, the destination can be full of hope, encouragement, peace, and wholeness. My prayer is that you will sense God's provision for you throughout your journey.

Kathy Baer
Director of Domestic Infant Adoption
Bethany Christian Services

acknowledgments

NO PROJECT LIKE this could have been completed with the willingness of so many to share their lives, their stories, and in most cases, their pain. It is truly impossible to thank each one who touched and contributed to this project. However, I would like to express my deepest appreciation to a number of people listed below. Some of them are professionals and volunteers from across this country who have, for decades, cared for and supported families facing an unplanned pregnancy. Thank you for the insights you shared with me as this project developed. Others are counselors and researchers who have informed us regarding the issues discussed in this book. Thank you for participating with such enthusiasm.

- Kathy Baer, director of Domestic Infant Adoption, Bethany Christian Services, Atlanta, Georgia
- Dr. Theresa Burke, Ph.D., founding director of Rachel's Vineyard and coauthor of *Forbidden Grief: The Unspoken Pain of Abortion*
- Nancy Caverlee, my daughter's mentor, Miami Valley Women's Center, Dayton, Ohio

- John Ensor, president of A Woman's Concern, Boston, Massachusetts
- Dr. Peggy Hartshorn, Ph.D., president, Heartbeat International, Columbus, Ohio
- Dr. Julie Parton, Ph.D., manager of the Crisis Pregnancy Ministry at Focus on the Family, Colorado Springs, Colorado
- Trudy Johnson, assistant editor, *HeartLink* newsletter, Focus on the Family, Crisis Pregnancy Ministry, and faculty member at Master's Graduate School of Divinity (Life Crisis Issue Department), Evansville, Indiana
- Dr. Charles Kenny, Ph.D., founder of Kenny & Associates, Inc. *The Right Brain People®*, Cordova, Tennessee
- Mary Martin Mason, author of *Out of the Shadows: Birthfathers' Stories*
- Debbie Nieport, director of development, Elizabeth's New Life Center, Dayton, Ohio, and her staff
- Anne and Jim Pierson, founders and directors of Loving and Caring, Inc., Lancaster, Pennsylvania
- Jim Pye, director of the Men's Ministry, Hope Pregnancy Centers of Brazos Valley, Texas
- Dr. David C. Reardon, Ph.D., director of the Elliot Institute, Springfield, Illinois
- Brenda Romanchik, director of Insight: Open Adoption Resources and Support, Royal Oak, Michigan
- Linda Schindler, executive director, Miami Valley Women's Center, Dayton, Ohio, and her staff

I also would like to say thank you to my developmental editor, Traci Mullins of Eclipse Editorial Services, who captured the vision for this project and has been an incredible support and encouragement. NavPress Publisher Dan Rich and Editorial Director Terry Behimer truly understood that this book needed to be written and offered their professional expertise and support. Thank you.

Deep gratitude to Karen LeBarr, whose invaluable help in making connections for me provided the foundation for much of this book.

acknowledgments

To West Carrollton, Ohio, Church of the Nazareen, our church family, for your love and support.

To Lynn Pettit, whose transcriptions of taped interviews were extremely valuable in the rush toward the deadline.

To my daughter, Kristy, whose journey unfolded within these pages— thank you for courageously sharing your story and for choosing life and doing the right thing.

To my son-in-law, Rick, for the caring husband and father you are to Micah and Annalise. We are very proud of both you and Kristy.

Finally, thank you to my husband, David, for your ever continued support, and to God, for continuing to open doors to new and broader experiences.

it wasn't supposed to be this way

A husband and wife planned and saved all of their lives for the trip of their dreams. They wanted to go to Italy. Carefully saving each spare dime or dollar, they prepared for the journey. They learned the language. They studied the culture. They purchased just the right clothes for the season they would be there. The day finally came and they boarded the plane. After many hours in the air, the flight attendant announced, "We will soon be landing. Welcome to Holland."

Startled, the woman frantically pushed the call button, shouting, "There's some mistake. We are supposed to be landing in Italy."

The flight attendant, attempting to calm the woman, explained, "This plane does not go to Italy."

Quite sure that they had simply erred when boarding the plane, the husband asked when the next plane would leave for Italy. The flight attendant replied, "Sir, I am sorry, there are no planes to Italy."

Disappointed beyond belief, the husband and wife looked at each other. "It wasn't supposed to be this way," they cried.

It wasn't supposed to be this way. Not in this story, which is shared often by Anne Pierson, founder of Loving and Caring.[1] "Holland" is not the place this couple planned to be. "Holland" is not the place where hundreds of thousands of parents facing an unplanned pregnancy with their daughter or son want to be either.

When a family learns of the pregnancy of their daughter or of their son's girlfriend, it is like they have arrived at a destination that is all wrong—not a place they planned to go, and certainly not a place where they wanted to stay. However, parents have two choices when they arrive in "Holland." They can remain disappointed, angry, and embittered, thus missing all that God has for them at this rerouted destination. Or they can, through God's mercy and grace, embrace all that God has for them as He is allowed to rebuild and restore the family.

In the process of writing this book, I had the privilege of sharing the stories of scores of parents who were just like us and of their teen or young adult children, just like our daughter Kristy. We were all on the same journey. None of us ever planned to be taking this road. I heard scores of stories of how God took the pain, disappointment, and confusion, and transformed it into hope and healing.

This book, which contains those stories, principles, insights, and advice, is crafted with the deep desire to provide hope, encouragement, and direction for parents and their child. The goal of *"Mom, Dad . . . I'm Pregnant"* is twofold: The first goal is to provide guidance to parents as they help their daughter or son make positive, godly decisions for the baby and for themselves. The second is to equip parents with the knowledge and tools they will need to make godly and positive decisions for themselves. Questions at the end of chapters are to help parents explore their feelings, concerns, and challenges in personal and practical ways. These questions can be answered by individual readers, but my prayer is that parents who are walking through a similar crisis will come together to read and discuss this book and share their experience, fears, and hopes. The support of others who really understand can provide the greatest strength and relief along this journey. Although the primary audience for this book is parents dealing with crisis pregnancies in their children, I hope it will also be a helpful resource for pregnancy resource centers, adoption agencies, pastors and church lay leaders, post-abortion support groups, and Christian college and high school libraries.

Several months ago I had the opportunity to meet with a number of birth grandparents—individuals and couples whose daughter or son made an adoption plan for their first grandchild. Before beginning the interview, one father, Rick Beggs, asked to open in prayer. What he prayed that morning reflects what I hope to accomplish with this book.

> *Heavenly Father, we are humbled by Your presence. We want to recognize You as the center of all of this. It is because of Your good will that we sit in this room today—not because of anything we have done or our kids have done, but because You choose us to be channels through which Your will might be presented and lived out before people You would like to draw to Yourself.*
>
> *We thank You, Lord, that we have our stories to share. A lot of times, there wasn't thankfulness in our hearts for what we have been through or are going through, but I know that You mean everything for our welfare and not for our calamity, so we rest in that truth today. If You can use our stories to point the way to You, we would be deeply thankful. May our words be Your words. In Jesus' name, amen.*

Rick's prayer captures the sentiments of hundreds of families who have walked this journey and willingly shared and supported one another. In the pages ahead you will journey with all of us through the struggle of myriad decisions that must be made. You will see how we learned so much about ourselves as parents and grandparents. You will also see how we learned about God as we experienced the truth that His grace is truly sufficient in *all* things. It is our prayer that within these pages you will find the hope and support you need even amid circumstances that cause your heart to cry out, "It wasn't supposed to be this way."

part one:

families forever changed

suddenly our whole world changed

1

ONE FAMILY'S JOURNEY

> When I heard the words, "Mom, I'm pregnant," I thought my life was over. I thought that this was the worst thing that could ever happen to us as a family. I have since learned that our life as a family wasn't over, but it has been forever changed.
>
> KATHERINE, A BIRTH GRANDMOTHER

WHEN OUR BEAUTIFUL twenty-one-year-old daughter came home from college on a spring Sunday afternoon in 1998, it appeared to be her usual drop-in-and-do-laundry visit. However, the real reason for her visit would propel us on a path of emotional turmoil, hurt, and confusion that we never expected to travel. We never expected to be here—not with her—not at this point in our family's life.

After returning from church that evening, Kristy sat down at the kitchen table and tearfully asked me to join her. "Mom, there is no easy way to tell you this. I'm pregnant," she quietly said. "Eight weeks, I think."

Too stunned too respond, all I could muster was, "Are you sure?"

"Yes, I'm sure. I took a pregnancy test and I have been so sick."

"Who knows?" I weakly asked.

"Sean does, but he won't speak to me," she said. "And Ray, Mom." It turned out that our son had known for a couple of weeks.

"I didn't mean for this to happen," Kristy whispered through painful tears. "I was foolish and careless."

I sat in dazed silence. *This can't be true.* I wanted to ask a million questions. "How could you have allowed this to happen?" "What were you thinking?" "What are you going to do now?" But I couldn't ask anything. Shocked, I sat looking at our child—a profoundly hurting, desperately frightened young lady—our daughter, our only daughter. My husband was yet to be told.

Just one hour earlier, I had been enjoying conversations with women at church, encouraging them in their Christian walk and laughing with them about family antics. All that seemed light years away now. Suddenly, it felt like my world crumbled around me. I didn't have any answers for my daughter at that moment. I didn't have answers for us.

After David arrived home, Kristy told him the news in the same hushed manner she had told me. His response—one of numbed disbelief—was similar to mine.

"As the news sank in," David recalled, "one part of me stayed in the kitchen, feeling the nauseating pain of what our daughter had just told me. Another part of me went away, thinking about all the issues and concerns we all would have to face. What we had supported, believed, and taught throughout our ministry—choose life—do the right thing—was no longer just a slogan or statement supporting the pro-life movement. It was a pronouncement that now touched us at the deepest, most personal level of our lives."

Some tense conversation followed. With nothing more to be said at that point, and the feeling of helplessness suffocating us, we all went our separate ways. Kristy, deciding not to return to school that evening, headed straight for her room and shut the door behind her. David, needing time and space, left to run an errand. I went to our room to prepare for bed. I could hear Kristy crying through her bedroom door. My heart was breaking for all of us.

David and I struggled with awkward conversation as that devastating evening finally ended. We attempted to sleep, but that luxury eluded us. For the first time in many, many years, I literally lay awake all night. Questions swirled around me. "What will be the future of this baby?" "What about Kristy's future?" "What about ours?" "Who do we tell, and when?"

Over the next several days we went numbly through the motions of returning to our work and carrying out our ministry responsibilities. Kristy returned to college. The journey was just beginning for us.

telling the news

Because David was the senior pastor of a large church, we were in an extremely difficult position. Our first concern, of course, was for our daughter; but at this early stage, still in shock, other concerns quickly emerged as well. David and I were both concerned how the church family would react. Would they still want us to continue in leadership under these conditions? Would they see us failing as parents? Would they still trust us? What would it feel like to be the subject of gossip? Would we have the emotional and psychological strength to continue meeting the demands of a vibrant, growing church amid such personal heartbreak and uncertainty?

After many hours of discussion, weighing the pros and cons of how we would proceed, we made a decision within the first weeks of learning about Kristy's pregnancy to talk with our church board as soon as possible. We did not want "the news" to trickle out, placing us and our church family in an awkward position. Following the regularly scheduled board meeting, my husband called me.

"It is time to come over," he told me. "I asked them to wait as we had something to share."

I walked in the board meeting room and sat next to my husband. In a calm manner, David related our news.

"For many years we have stood by you and your families in crisis. We now face our own. We need to share with you tonight about a family situation. Kristy just told us within the last several days that she is pregnant. We want to apologize to the church for any embarrassment this might bring. We will respond to whatever you ask us to do regarding our future leadership here. All we do ask of you is that you allow us time as a family to regroup and begin to work through the issues that face us."

As we turned to leave, some of the board members stood and walked toward us. We were surrounded with words of encouragement, prayers for wisdom, and hugs of support.

The following Sunday, I faced another difficult moment. I taught an adult women's Sunday school class. Through the years, the class cared for each other through various crises. We all had experienced God's provision in trying and tragic circumstances. I knew the class's history of loving support and maturity, but I still dreaded telling them our news. As the hour drew to a close, I ended the lesson early.

"My friends," I told them. "We have laughed together, cried together, prayed together over the last three years. It has brought healing to all of us. However, I need to tell you that our family is now entering a place where we have never been. Our daughter, who many of you know, is pregnant. We wanted you to know so that you wouldn't hear the rumor and wonder why I had said nothing. We don't know what the days ahead will bring. I know that we have talked a lot and encouraged each other with the knowledge that God's grace is sufficient. I believe that God will teach me at a deeper level what that means in the months to come."

What followed here, just as with our earlier announcement, were expressions of love, acceptance, and encouragement. What I had feared—church gossip and rejection—never materialized. In fact it was quite the opposite. Sitting one afternoon at a church luncheon, I talked openly with one of our ladies about Kristy, assuming she had heard. She began to tear up and said, "I didn't know that, no one told me." Kristy was well into her sixth month by then.

riding the roller coaster

In the early weeks following the disclosure of this news, I felt as though I had stepped onto an emotional roller coaster, and with every heart-stopping curve I encountered a new or recurring emotion . . . guilt, grief, loss, anger, rejection, fear, despair, hurt, sorrow. The ride jostled me from every side. My husband experienced a similar emotional assault.

GUILT

Guilt was the first emotion that rose to the surface as the reality of our situation hit home. I felt as though I had failed Kristy as her mother. For a period of time, guilt became my constant companion. My mind constantly rehearsed: *What went wrong? What did I do to cause her behavior? What didn't I do? How can I fix this since I am to blame?*

A close cousin to guilt is "if-onlys." If only I had been more attentive. If only I had spent more time with her. If only I had allowed her more freedom. If only I had not been so rigid about some things. If only I hadn't smothered her as a parent. If only, if only . . .

David, too, was tormented. "I kept asking myself, would this have been different if I had listened more—if I had been home more," David related. "We knew during Kristy's adolescence that she was struggling with a lot of issues. She kept her heart walled off from us, and I continually asked myself, 'What if I had been more competent to reach her? Would we be here dealing with this?'"

GRIEF

I think at the heart of a family crisis of this nature is the sense of loss and the accompanying grief that follows. It was for us. One of our bedrooms serves as the memory wall for generations of family photos. One particular frame contains pictures of Kristy's growing-up years. When I walked into that room and glanced at those happy, carefree, smiling faces of a three-year-old, ten-year-old, thirteen-year-old, overwhelming emotions of loss and sadness rose up within me.

Memories of happier days flooded me. I remembered the joy we had watching our daughter's basketball games during her junior high and high school days. I wouldn't miss a game. She was an assertive rebounder and won county-wide honors. I recalled the excitement we all felt when she was chosen from nationally conducted interviews as a counselor-in-training for Kids-Across-America camps, a Christian inner-city program in Missouri. Kristy has a heart for inner-city kids, and in those late high school and early college days, God provided summer outlets for ministry both in Missouri and Ohio. She was invigorated by living out her dreams. But now she was traveling a different road.

Occasionally, I would sit down on the edge of the bed and cry—grieving the losses—loss of the dream of what "should" have been:

- Her innocence
- Enjoying her college graduation
- Watching her dreams of ministry emerge
- Seeing the wonder of her falling in love with the right man
- Planning a wedding
- Anticipating the birth of a grandchild under happy circumstances

Our grieving was also for Kristy—for her losses and struggles—now and in the future. In the midst of your own hurt, anger, and pain, you can't help but feel fear and desperation for the child to whom you've given your heart and life.

SHAME

Although we knew we had the support of our church family, facing them each week in ministry capacities proved to be difficult. David found stepping into the pulpit each Sunday even more emotionally demanding than he expected it to be.

"I felt that I had lost my credibility. It was very difficult to continue to function in those early days. It was incredibly challenging to face the congregation each week. How could I talk to other families about their spiritual and emotional issues when we were facing such a mountain of concerns within our own family? How could I help them when such deep hurt was shackled to me?"

What engaged our imagination most during those early weeks of deep pain and disappointment was the fantasy of flight. "Why don't we take a sabbatical for a period of time," we asked ourselves. Withdrawing temporarily from all our responsibilities was tempting to us. We felt that in so doing we would have time to work through our issues and concerns with Kristy and the soon-to-be born child alone and out of the public view.

We actually drove over to a neighboring community to look at available housing. We knew that following through on that decision would ultimately mean David would have to resign his position as the senior pastor, as our church did not have a sabbatical option. This flight plan, however, was not

God's plan. In the midst of this fantasy of flight, a young pastoral friend of David's, Jamie Johnson, dropped by his office. We now believe he was sent there by God. In their conversation, this young pastor challenged David.

"You are not finished here," Jamie told David. "You are not going to walk away from your calling. You are not going to end your ministry like this. When you do finish, you need to finish strong."

It felt like a profound admonishment from the Lord to David. Calling me after Jamie left his office he echoed his words, "We are not going to run from this. We are not going to finish like this. Whenever we are done here, we will finish strong!"

LONELINESS

For families in crisis who also serve in leadership roles, finding a trusted, listening ear feels out of reach. We felt, as do many other pastoral families in crisis, that we really couldn't or shouldn't talk to anyone in the church. This perception brought a deep sense of being very alone. Fears of betrayal, concerns of a judgmental response, or loss of respect blocked that source of support.

After the initial shock of disclosure, I found myself desperately needing to share what was happening in our lives. Talking with my husband was helpful, but he was hurting too. I was convinced that a confidante needed to be outside our church.

I contacted a local counselor, who was also a pastor's wife. I went with great anticipation of hearing words that would sustain me in the coming months. That didn't happen. I am not really sure to this day how the conversation moved in the direction it did, but we spent almost the entire hour discussing her challenging role as pastor's wife. Very little dialogue touched where I was and why I was there. As the hour ended, she said, "Don't think about paying me today, I just enjoyed our talk."

That was it. The session was over. I went out to my car and cried. I needed an outlet for the whirl of thoughts and feelings inside of me. Now who would I talk to?

I didn't realize at the time that God had always intended my support to be from friends who were right there in front of me. There were Pat and Robin Shadowens, a mother and daughter who had journeyed this way more than a decade earlier. I felt drawn to them in a desperate need to speak out loud the confusion I was experiencing. There was Marcia Southerland, an incredible woman with the gift of mercy who just seemed to know the right words at the right time. Then there was the time John and Kelly Bayse and I met for lunch. They asked good questions about feelings, thoughts, and plans for all of us.

What was amazing to me in those early days was the healing that was beginning to take place in my heart. Their comments of understanding began to quietly soothe open sores of woundedness and hurt: "We've been there," "This is a detour, but you, David, Kristy, and the one to come will make it," "Your pain will not last forever." One particular comment brought hope: "When you see your grandchild for the very first time, you will experience a whole new level of love." That thought brought hope for all of us.

ACCEPTANCE

David, in particular, and I, to some degree, had worked with hundreds of individuals and families in crisis. We both knew from our professional lives that people go through stages from denial to anger to grief and loss to acceptance and beyond. I don't believe that we spent too much time in the denial stage. We did experience flares of anger and resentment about being hurled into such a circumstance. Those feelings came and went. However, we did linger in grief and loss for a while. But as God enabled us through His Word and through the support of those around us, we both eventually moved into the acceptance stage. With that came the realization that our daughter needed us at a far deeper level than ever before.

That acceptance meant that we would walk this journey with her—to the doctor's appointments, to the maternity store for clothes, to Lamaze classes and child-care classes. That acceptance meant that this situation was no longer all about *our* feelings, losses, and disappointment, but about Kristy and the child to come. That acceptance also meant that, at some level, we would be empathically experiencing what she was going through.

walking alongside

"Mom, Sean won't call me back," Kristy told me one afternoon. "I just needed to talk with him about all of this and he won't call me back. What can I do?"

I sat across from her at the familiar kitchen table having no answers. Sean denied his involvement and basically told her it was entirely her problem. I didn't know what it felt like to be abandoned. It had never happened to me. I didn't know what it felt like to hold broken, empty promises. I could only imagine as I looked into her eyes. I felt at such a loss.

With each Christmas season came a tradition for us—young girls from our church came to the parsonage to decorate cookies. Although Kristy's due date was within two weeks, and things were uncertain, we carried on as usual. One evening nearly fifty young girls (in two shifts!) filled the kitchen and dining room with chatter and laughter.

Kristy had moved back home at the end of the school term. Tired from semester exams, tired of being pregnant, and wanting to just stay out of the "creative confusion," she stayed in her room. I didn't see her all evening.

After the last cookie had been decorated and the last plate wrapped, the children left. A few adults stayed behind to help clean up and then soon left. As I went down the hall, I could hear Kristy crying from her room. I lightly tapped on the door.

"Come in, Mom," she whispered.

I went over and sat down on her bed, the same way I had done hundreds of times while she was growing up. "Honey, what's going on?" I asked her, wondering if something had happened—maybe a phone call or something.

"Mom, I know the girls didn't know I was in here," she began. "Some of them were standing outside my door talking about me. They just kept talking. 'Did you hear she is pregnant? She's not married. Can you believe that?' It went on and on. It was horrible to hear them."

Again, I was at a place with her that I had never been. I didn't know what it felt like to hear people talk about me. I didn't know what it felt like to wonder what other people were thinking and saying. All I could do that night was just hold her, perhaps more tightly than ever before.

One of pregnancy's earliest milestones is the trip to the doctor for the ultrasound. Is the baby a girl or boy? What an exciting moment! But Kristy and I would experience it alone—at least without the father of her baby there. Sean had made that perfectly clear.

When she was five months along, the doctor offered the opportunity for the ultrasound. Kristy made the appointment and I drove. My daughter hardly looked pregnant as she prepared for the procedure.

"It looks like we have a little boy," the tech said. "He has all ten fingers, ten toes, and everything looks just fine. Any questions?"

A boy . . . *a boy!* No longer just "the baby." Now a grandson—Micah Benjamin—the name Kristy had chosen. What had my friend said about experiencing a whole new level of love? It was already happening.

decision-making under duress

The day after Kristy told us of her situation, she returned to school. We knew that some decisions needed to be made right away—others, more complex and difficult, could wait. Most of those decisions were Kristy's to make.

As a young adult, she needed to be responsible for a lot of reasons. Most important, she was capable of making those decisions. I wanted to step in and take control, hoping perhaps to regain some sense of being able to fix this. But that would have been the worst thing I could have done. Decision making needed to belong to my daughter. Kristy's pregnancy didn't wipe away those character qualities that we had seen demonstrated in her life before. Her pregnancy would require that she develop them at a deeper level.

In our case, because Kristy was twenty-one and a college student, some of those short-term decisions included:

- Could she and would she finish out this school term?
- Would she stay on campus or move home and commute during the pregnancy?
- Would she continue to work?

- What doctor would she see?
- Who did she want to tell about the situation?
- How did she want us to handle the situation with our friends and others?

As the newness of our situation settled, we watched as Kristy made those decisions that demonstrated to us some very important character qualities. Kristy not only finished that spring term, but continued through summer school and into the fall, so that after her child's birth, she would only have one quarter of college to finish. (She returned to finish that last quarter only five days after her son's birth.)

She stayed in her campus apartment and decided to move home four weeks before her due date. She continued working as a waitress until it was physically impossible and then took a job as a receptionist in a nursing home. She asked her primary doctor for a referral to a doctor who would care for her during the pregnancy and took care of making appointments. She gradually began telling her friends and encouraged us to talk with those who could offer support.

During Kristy's fourth and fifth months of pregnancy, the question as to the baby's future obviously came up. We didn't talk a whole lot about it as a family, only when Kristy would bring it up. We assured her that we would support any decision that she made.

I know that she was weighing her options very carefully. Her mentor at the Miami Valley Women's Center in Dayton, Ohio, whom Kristy sought out for support, was a tremendous listener. I think it was far easier for Kristy to explore all her feelings with her than with us, and that was okay.

Nancy Caverlee, her mentor, suggested that the three of us visit with another pastor's daughter who had almost the identical experience as Kristy. Michelle initially had made an adoption plan, but later changed her mind and decided to parent her daughter. A couple of years following the birth of her child, Michelle met and married a youth pastor who adopted her daughter. Nancy thought it would be good for us to talk with her about the issues she faced in making the decision she did.

Kristy asked good questions that evening as the three of us sat in Michelle's living room. "How hard was doing this alone for you?" "How did you make the final decision to parent?" "What are some things I need to know about doing this by myself?" During the course of the evening, I noticed the struggle in our daughter subside. I could see from her countenance that she had made a decision. At that point, I didn't know what it was. I just knew it had been made.

On the way home from Michelle's, Kristy cautiously said, "I have made my decision. I am going to parent my baby. I graduate three months after he is born. I know it will be hard, but after much prayer and thought, this is the decision. I know I can do it. I just know we will be all right."

a gift from heaven

An early morning voice at our bedroom door startled me awake.

"Mom, Mom, something's going on," Kristy called out. "I am really hurting and sick. Do you think these are labor pains?"

I bolted out of bed, had her sit down, and asked a few more "diagnostic" questions. It definitely was time to head for the hospital.

What day is it? I thought to myself. *This is the day our grandchild will be born.* It was December 29, 1998. As we pulled out of the driveway, I glanced at the clock; it was 6:00 AM.

We quickly drove to the maternity emergency section of the hospital, checked Kristy in and began the wait. We were surprised to be told that she was quite far along in the labor process. It looked like our grandson would be born soon. Kristy, a cross country runner in college, had taken good care of herself during the pregnancy, walking a couple of miles most days, even in cold weather. Her hard work paid off. Micah was born just before 1:00 PM after a short seven hours of labor.

When we held Micah within moments of his birth, David and I both were overwhelmed with love for him and compassion for his mother. Kristy and Micah came home two days after his birth. It was a snowy New Year's Eve. All of us were exhausted by the events of the week and welcomed a quiet evening at home.

As 1998 slipped away and 1999 entered, I looked into the living room at our daughter, sound asleep on the floor in front of the fireplace. Beside her, cozy in his infant carrier, was Micah, sleeping peacefully. The past year had brought much unexpected pain and hurt. The New Year looked hopeful. We had finished traveling this part of the journey. New and challenging days would lie ahead, we knew that. But as a family we had come so far.

That evening and hundreds of evenings since then, I look at Micah's bright face and mischievous smile with such thanksgiving. We have all been changed—forever changed—with the coming of this little one. We have learned much about God—His love, His compassion, His enablement, and His grace.

responding to the crisis

SEVEN THINGS PARENTS NEED TO KNOW

> After the initial news that Jason's girlfriend was pregnant, we were angry, disappointed, and deeply hurt by his choices. However, we knew that for the sake of Jason, Krissy, and the baby to come, we couldn't stay there. We had to move beyond our own feelings to be able to support the kids through this. And in time, we were able to do that.
>
> BRUCE, JASON'S DAD

"KINDRA HAD BEEN avoiding us for several days," Dean said quietly as he recalled the "telling moment."

"She would come home from school and slip away into her room. She was spending way too much time in her room, away from the family. She complained of not feeling well, but if we inquired, she would get defensive and change the subject. I had waited long enough. Finally one evening, I tapped on her door and asked if I could come in.

"What are you doing?" I asked.

Huddled over her desk in a dim room she responded, "Writing a letter."

"To whom? Anyone we know?" I asked.

"You and Mom," she whispered.

"What about?"

No answer. After a very long pause I blurted out, "What about, Kindra? Are you pregnant?" For a number of months I had been carrying a nagging sense that something like this was coming.

"Just read the letter," she replied.

Taking the letter from her hand I decided to read it alone. My wife was gone for a few hours, and if the letter was about what I had suspected, I knew I would need time to process it. I went to my den and shut the door.

> Dear Dad and Mom,
> I don't know how to tell you this in person, so I am writing you this letter. I need to tell you that I am pregnant. Two months, I think. I don't know what else to say or to write. My friends said you needed to know. So now I have told you.
> I'm sorry,
> Kindra

"I sat there numb," Dean said. "We knew her lifestyle choices could lead to this, but I think we kept thinking . . . *it couldn't happen to us.*"

the telling moment

Life-changing news just like the kind Dean received propels thousands of families into a confusing and gut-wrenching experience. What has the telling moment felt like to other families?

OVERWHELMING

For Amy's parents, Mary and Tony, the news of the pregnancy just added more pain to what they were already feeling. They had struggled with their daughter's rebellion and drug use.

"Before all this happened, we were already dealing with the feelings of guilt for the bad choices that Amy was making," Tony explained. "She was into drugs and drinking—we knew that."

"When she moved to Florida, I knew her continuing poor choices could create this problem," Mary added. "She didn't call home very much, so when I picked up the phone and heard her voice, I just knew one of two things had happened—either she was in trouble with the police or she was pregnant."

Continuing, Mary said, "Her first words to me were, 'Mom, I'm pregnant, but I am not considering an abortion. Can I come home?'"

I said, "Of course. But are you sure?"

"Yes, Mom, I have taken five pregnancy tests," Amy told me.

"We talked for a while, and I recall just trying to remember to breathe and make sense on the telephone. I could hear how upset she was. We got through the conversation and made arrangements for her to come home."

Following that call from Amy, the next call Mary made was to her mother.

"All I could get out was 'Mom'," Mary said.

"Did someone die?" she asked. "Honey, what happened?"

"We just got a call from Amy. She said she is pregnant," Mary reluctantly told her. "What is the family going to say?" Mary asked. "I have worked so hard to be the perfect family. This was not how it was supposed to play out. What am I going to do?"

Mary's mother listened and finally said gently, "Mary, for the first time in your life, you cannot change this, you cannot fix it. All you can do is trust in the Lord."

"How is God going to work this out?" Mary asked her mom. "It just seems too big—even for God."

HEARTBREAKING

The telling moment for Rick and Nancy broke their hearts. Like all parents who face the news of an unplanned pregnancy in their young adult child, all they could think about was that this wasn't what they ever imagined they would be dealing with.

"Sarah had been home from school during the Christmas break and complained of not feeling well," Nancy shared. "She returned to school to begin the second semester. It was the end of January that she called and told us she was pregnant."

Some parents like Nancy reported having a sense that the news they were about to hear was coming. It was as if God was preparing them ahead of time.

"It was interesting the morning she called," Nancy said. "During devotions I felt impressed that Sarah was pregnant, but I didn't say anything to

Rick. I didn't want to alarm him. I went to breakfast with a friend and told her that I thought Sarah was pregnant. I just felt it in my spirit.

"That night we got a call from a good friend and administrator at Sarah's school. I answered, and he asked me to get Rick on the phone too. Right then, I knew what he was going to say."

"There is a possibility that Sarah is pregnant," our friend told us. He had heard it from his daughter who was Sarah's close friend. Rick called Sarah right away and confronted her. That call took Rick to a place he had never been.

"When I called Sarah that night I asked her how she was doing. She had been sick, which was another reason Nancy felt that she was pregnant. We chitchatted a moment about how she felt, and then I asked straight out, 'Sarah, are you pregnant?' I didn't want to mess around; I wanted to know."

"Well, sort of, kind of . . . yes and no," she replied. Sarah had had conflicting pregnancy test results.

During that first phone call between Sarah and Rick there were a lot of tears and anger. Later that week Rick was in Chicago at a business meeting. He would slip out to check messages to see if Sarah had called him with any news. When the pregnancy was finally verified, Rick remembers just sitting out in the lobby of the hotel and feeling heartbroken. "Both of us just cried on the phone," he said. "It was an incredibly emotional moment."

These families, like thousands of others, were just beginning a journey that would impact them for the rest of their lives. What did they most need to know to get them over the many hurdles that lay ahead?

NEED TO KNOW ONE: Parents will experience myriad painful and confusing emotions.

As the initial shock of the news begins to wear off, innumerable painful emotions follow. They certainly did for us. When Kristy told us her news, we did not know how to navigate through our own emotions. As time went on, more knowledge about what to expect regarding this personal journey gave us a sense of support and realization that others had walked this way and come out okay on the other side. What are those emotions that we and others encountered?

FEELINGS OF FAILURE AND GUILT

Two of the most intense emotions that come to the surface early are feelings of failure and guilt.

"We had been planning this special family outing for just the three of us for a number of weeks," Jill shared. "Katie had been so busy with her senior year high school activities and we felt that we were losing touch with her. We thought this brief weekend would be a great time to reconnect.

"Katie got into the back seat of the car as we prepared to leave. She was very quiet, so Ed and I just talked to each other up front. Suddenly Katie sat up between us. She quietly told us that she was pregnant. She just said it. The whole reason for the weekend suddenly changed," Jill recalled, "from relaxing together to dealing with this shocking news. I was almost immediately flooded with the 'if-onlys.' If only we had become Christians sooner; if only we had been stricter; if only we had loved her more; if only we had paid more attention to who she was dating. The 'if-onlys' were innumerable, and we soon understood that continuing down that path was leading us into guilt and blame. It provided no solutions, just pain."

FEELINGS OF INTENSE ANGER

For John and Catherine, the depth of their anger caught them off guard.

"Rachel's unplanned pregnancy came as the result of a way of life we knew about and were heartbroken over," John explained. "She went from one sexual relationship to another. When she told us of the situation, I didn't know I could experience such incredible anger."

"It was such a strange gamut of emotions," Catherine added, "as I sat looking at this daughter we loved so deeply and yet had hurt us so deeply. I can just remember saying to her, 'Living the way you did had affected only you, but now all that has changed.' We were filled with uncomfortable and unfamiliar confusion. This is a path upon which we have never walked. We did not know how to deal with the feelings we were experiencing," Rachel's mom concluded.

Anger is an emotion that Greg, Rebecca's father, still struggles with at some level. He admits that he hasn't yet forgiven the birth father. "Forgiveness would have been much easier if he had come to us and taken some form of responsibility," Greg explained. "But he simply walked away, leaving Rebecca alone, confused, and deeply hurt."

Rick's anger over his daughter's pregnancy eventually took him to a place where God touched him and taught him.

"I was furious," Rick said. "This felt like a big hit on us. I had been one of thirteen people that ran a national family ministry. I had been chosen as one of the top one hundred alumni at the school where Sarah was attending. Every success was a one-on-top-of another, and so would the ramifications of this news as it trickled down. Initially this was a pride issue for me: How was I going to be viewed?

"It took me about a week to ten days to work through the anger and disappointment so I could start to see the bigger picture. That is when I first began sensing God's presence in the middle of it. It was as if God would whisper, 'What about you? Who do you think you are? Sure, this sin is going to be exterior, but what about your interior? What about your sins? What about who you are before Me? What about My grace that covers you?'

"This situation was no longer about me—my ego and reputation," Rick concluded.

FEELINGS OF DEEP SADNESS AND LOSS

Most parents, as their youthful daughters move into late adolescence and young adulthood, dream about the day when their daughter meets just the right person and makes plans for that perfect wedding day. When pregnancy occurs in the life of a young woman, for her parents that dream suddenly seems dead. It did for us because Kristy herself felt that a bright, happy future was now so far out of reach for her.

Other losses emerge as well, such as the joys of watching a high school or college graduation, or of anticipating the arrival of the first grandchild (under "right" conditions). Deep feelings of loss accumulate as parents helplessly watch their daughter experience the consequences of her pregnancy.

"It was very difficult for me, as Rebecca's dad, to watch her experience one loss after another," Greg shared. "She was just getting established in a brand-new career, in a state she had always wanted to live in, her dream place . . . that was all gone. She couldn't stay there alone so far from home with no family support. The big thing that took me awhile to understand was her mourning over her relationship with the baby's father. I didn't realize the deep love she had for Rob.

"My wife reminded me that while Rebecca was going through all the uncertainty about whether or not to make an adoption plan, she still felt that Rob was the one she was going to marry. When she told him of her plan to keep the baby, he abruptly informed her that their relationship was over. It took her at least the first year to move on from that loss—grieving the tremendous rejection and loss of someone she thought she was going to spend her life with."

For Sherrie, watching her husband grieve brought a double sense of loss.

"Don went into a deep mourning for the dreams that were now lost to our daughter. The summer before her senior year in high school, she had plans to take a leadership position at a Christian summer camp—a position for which she applied and was accepted. Don knew how her heart was breaking over her unwise choice of having premarital sex. He wanted to fix it for her, but it was a journey she had to take. I wanted to fix his pain as well, but of course only God could do that."

NEED TO KNOW TWO: Your daughter or son is journeying to a place where she or he has never been. Your response and support are critical.
Circumstances surrounding an unplanned pregnancy are as varied as the story of each young man and young woman. However, each faces similar tasks. They will have to share the secret.

For a young woman, the first task is to deal with the reality of the pregnancy. When she flings her fourth positive pregnancy test into the wastebasket, she may also feel that she is tossing away her future. Plans for college or dreams of a bright career after college are potentially wiped away by the looming crisis. From the first frightening, suspicious moment, a young birth mother's life is forever changed.

How do many young women view their pregnancy? As a threat, according to Rev. Curt Young, author of *The Missing Piece: Adoption Counseling in Pregnancy Resource Centers*.

> When we asked women to visualize the moment that they discovered they were pregnant, most said that they were surprised, shocked, amazed, and confused. The language of crisis and threat was used. At the emotional level, they responded as if they have no idea where babies come from. This emotional response may allow them to play the victims of circumstance, rather than deal with the fact that they have made a bad decision. Their decisions about pregnancy are driven by emotion, not reason. Particularly when the choice is abortion, the decision is made prior to any consideration for the unborn child. The choice of abortion is more akin to a reflexive response to a threat.[1]

A young woman's unexpected pregnancy potentially throws her world into chaos. She is having an unplanned baby at an inopportune time and under far less than ideal conditions. For a young man, the announcement of the pregnancy brings him face to face with the consequences of his choice to be sexually active. What he thought was fun now isn't fun anymore. During those early days of pregnancy, what erupts for many young women and men is shock, denial, disbelief, and fear.

Denial was seventeen-year-old Janet's first defense mechanism.

"I tried to deny it to myself, at first. This couldn't have happened to me," Janet proclaimed. "I'd wake up in the middle of the night thinking I was having a bad dream, but then reality would hit me. I would be sick every morning and lived in fear that my parents would hear me."

Denial is part of the initial reaction for young men as well. Josh's response of denial and fear mirrors many.

"When Sandi told me about the pregnancy, I was really scared. I had just started my sophomore year in college. She was a senior in high school. This couldn't be happening! I finally realized that it was true. My parents drove over with me to tell Sandi's parents. Dad had to stop the car two or three times so I could throw up. I was just so scared about what was ahead."

When faced with the overwhelming circumstances of an unplanned pregnancy, a parent's response is critical. Yes, anger, disappointment, and fear are normal and to be expected. But after the shock, the message that emerges over time will have long-term implications.

Tony, Amy's dad, walked his way through anger and loss. In a matter of several weeks, he realized that his daughter needed something from him, in particular. "It was important for Amy to know that we still loved her. The pregnancy, although a disappointment, didn't change that for us. We told her that we wanted her to come home, and we would work through this together. I affirmed her decision to not consider an abortion. Amy and I had participated in pro-life marches; she had always been exposed to that. She could have easily had an abortion in Florida, and we would have never known. As she moved through the decision-making process and made an adoption plan for her baby, we affirmed her way of working through this difficult time."

Young men involved in an unplanned pregnancy need the same support. Josh's dad Kyle said, "When Josh told us that Sandi was pregnant, of course we went through all the initial emotions. However, Josh was stepping up to his responsibilities, and we encouraged him to do so. His poor choices forced him to look at the life he was leading—totally ignoring what he knew to be right—and what God wanted for him. He is making great progress in growing up, and he needs to hear that from us. One important thing is that after he and Sandi made a decision to place their son for adoption, they asked us to be part of choosing a family. We knew that this decision was a painful one for them, as it was for us. But it was made in the best interest of that precious little one."

NEED TO KNOW THREE: Fathers and mothers may deal with this family crisis in totally different ways, potentially leaving one parent feeling alone and unsupported.

A crucial area of concern when this crisis hits home is the challenge to communicate about it at all.

"We hardly talked about it," Mary explained. "It was all so painful. I could hardly talk to Tony because I was hurting so badly. How can two wounded people help each other? It's like two medics caring for each other on the battlefield."

Sometimes, actions and feeling don't match. That's what Margie and Ken discovered months into their daughter's pregnancy.

"My husband didn't share his feelings in the beginning," shared Margie, "but later told me that the pregnancy was a real stumbling block in his walk of faith." Together we had been praying that God would place a hedge of protection around both our children. We felt that April had made such progress in her personal faith walk. After going through a bit of a rebellious stage in high school, she was really coming back to be the girl we had always loved. She was now attending a Christian college and deepening her faith. When the pregnancy happened, Ken got angry at God. He felt that God hadn't answered his prayers to protect his daughter. He didn't express that feeling for months into the experience."

Continuing, Margie said, "When he finally shared that with me after the baby was born, I had the opposite reaction. I felt that this *was* a protection of sorts. I thought, *What if April had continued in this sexual relationship and hadn't gotten pregnant and continued this course from one sexual relationship to another?* This pregnancy stopped her cold. She had to ask herself what was important in life. What was she going to choose? What was she going to do now? She chose to be a wife and mother."

Ken's resolution of this spiritual challenge came after the wedding and after the baby was born. "Once he saw how happy they were together and began to have a better relationship with April's husband, he began to see this as a blessing," Marge said. "Looking back, I would have done some things differently. We didn't talk about our feelings. Ken was good at covering up his emotions, and I didn't know what he was really feeling. Superficially it looked like we were in sync. I would have asked Ken more explicitly about his feelings, but I thought I knew what they were. His actions said one thing, but I later learned he felt differently. Ken's reactions of supporter and provider for April masked his own feelings of hurt and disappointment," she concluded.

Much like this couple, Dean and Brenda lived out the experience of their daughter's pregnancy in different ways. Eighteen-year-old Kindra's news brought a flood of emotions, from shame, disbelief, and embarrassment, to deep hurt. However, Kindra's mother and father had totally opposite responses.

"Men and women just don't express things the same," Brenda commented. "I needed to talk, but Dean didn't. He was never much of a talker, especially about feelings, and he surely wasn't when this happened. I didn't know what he was thinking or feeling about what was happening to our family. However, that changed in a very unexpected way.

"Dean was always doing little remodeling projects around the house, but right after this happened he started a major one. Kindra told us right after Christmas, and then she moved out to live with her child's birth father. Dean began a project that I knew would never end. He completely tore up two bedrooms and a bathroom downstairs. I don't like disorder, plus we have a lot of ADHD in our family; I thought Dean was just 'ADHDing' with these projects. I felt like he was running away from me.

"One afternoon his appearance in the family room jolted me to a reality—he was deeply hurting over this. He came into the room in tears and said, 'I don't know what happened. I was just minding my own business downstairs and all of a sudden a thought about Kindra would come—and boom—look at me, I'm a mess.'"

Brenda continued. "All this time I was thinking that he was just making an incredible mess down there, and it was probably never going to get finished. That was far from the truth. This activity was an outlet for his emotions. Perhaps this was his attempt to reorder our physical world when our emotional world was in such chaos. He could actually control the outcome of this . . . while he couldn't the other. He did work on that project the whole time during the pregnancy . . . and he finished it!"

Dean commented, "I never thought about it being an outlet until Brenda said that. I just went down there one day and thought, *I don't like these doors. I am ripping them out.* I guess I didn't like what was happening in our home and this was one thing I could fix. I was in charge of that."

"I think men, especially, have to do something physically with the anger they are feeling," Brenda asserted. "I was sharing this experience with another woman who had been through the same experience. When I told her about what Dean was doing she started to laugh. She told me that her husband, Chuck, had gone outside one day with a chain saw. He was going to saw down a tree branch that was bugging him . . . he was just sawing and sawing away at the branch. Finally a neighbor came over and asked, 'Chuck, do you really want to cut that branch down? If you do, it's going to fall on your house.' Chuck just quit sawing, walked back in the house, and put the saw away."

Another potentially serious tension that occasionally arises is the double bind felt by one parent—most often the mother. Mothers of young women experiencing an unplanned pregnancy often feel caught in the middle between a hurting, desperate daughter and a hurting, angry husband. They want to love and nurture their hurting, frightened child while maneuvering through the emotions and reactions of their husband. One woman commented at a support group meeting for young girls and their mothers, "I am taking care of my daughter through this. I am trying to manage my husband's anger and frustration. But who is going to take care of me and what I am feeling? I am feeling so torn and so alone."

NEED TO KNOW FOUR: Parents will need to find a balance between supporting their young adult and letting her take responsibility.

While one mistake a parent can make is withholding support from their child, another mistake is giving her too much support. According to Dr. Julie Parton, manager of the Crisis Pregnancy Ministry at Focus on the Family, "Some parents simply move in and take over. They make all the medical appointments, doctors' appointments, offer to babysit full time. What often happens with these girls is that they are right back in the clinic the next year facing another unplanned pregnancy. Why? Because they fail to pay a price when the parents take over and do too much."

If a daughter chooses to parent her baby, Dr. Parton's advice is that her parents say, "We don't want to deny you the privilege of being a parent in the fullest sense of the word. You will be the parent of this child—totally, in every way—emotionally, physically, financially. We will be the grandparents."

Dr. Parton notes that it is difficult to find a balance between supporting one's daughter appropriately and not supporting her at all. She shared a story of a family that she felt did it "right."

One afternoon a mother and daughter came into our clinic for a pregnancy test. It was obvious to me that theirs was a pretty wealthy family. During the course of our interview I felt that we established a good relationship. This was a Christian family, and the young lady was finishing her second year of college. We spent a lot of time laying out a plan of action for the future. As they got up to go the mother said to me, "I have one more thing I need to ask you." The young lady said good-bye to me and went out to the car. I saw her talking on a cell phone. Her mother noticed that too and told me what her daughter was doing: She was making her first Medicaid appointment. Her mother said to me, "We could completely pay for all her expenses, but she needs to be responsible. She wants to be a mother to her baby, and we want her to be that in every way."

Finding the balance between supporting and enabling required another family to make a plan and stick to it.

"After Amy came back home, it was hard not to hover over her and continue to rescue her," Mary said. "It was a constant mental challenge. Tony and I would run back to our bedroom and bark at each other. 'You weren't supposed to do that,' one of us would say. Then we'd have to remind each other: 'Remember, *this* is what we decided to do.' We had to stay firm in our resolve. We had decided things ahead of time, like letting Amy find her own doctor. We made it clear that we couldn't afford to pay her medical bills; we have no insurance. We challenged her with, 'What are you going to do?' She came back to me and said she had been to the Medicaid office and had the names of three doctors she was going to interview. 'I would like you to come with me to my first appointment,' she said. That floored me—it was so grown up and responsible."

Other decisions Amy's parents made in advance included communicating to her that she had to get a job and pay rent. Reality hit Amy hard at first: This would not be a free ride. "But this was our home," Mary said, "and Amy was coming back to live with us after two years on her own. She had to comply with our rules, and she would have responsibilities. The fact that we had enjoyed our lifestyle as empty nesters made it easier to impose some requirements and boundaries. She was angry at first. She didn't want to face reality . . . but she did!"

NEED TO KNOW FIVE: Parents and their child will need to decide who, when, and how to tell family and friends.

In the early days of Kristy's pregnancy, we knew that we faced many hurdles. One of those hurdles, as I mentioned in the first chapter, was to tell our church board and church family. With Kristy's permission and knowledge, we did just that. This was followed by a gradual telling of family and friends.

Who to tell, when, and how, is a hurdle faced by every parent in the midst of an unplanned pregnancy.

Mary and Tony told Amy that they would wait until she wanted to let people know. When she was ready, she had to do the telling. Tony explained, "That included telling the family—the grandparents and other family members. There had to be consequences."

Another dad, Rick, felt the same way. "We weren't going to do the telling to family members, including Sarah's younger brother. Sarah was. She accepted that responsibility and understood that she had to be the one to do it."

The challenge to tell, for some, is handled in a completely different way. For Brenda, talking about it was the last thing she wanted to do. "I just couldn't talk about it much," she said. "It would just ruin me." The less said, the fewer the awkward questions, she reasoned. As a massage therapist, Brenda would go to work and "just escape." She was used to helping other people. "Part of me just didn't want to be the problem," she explained. "I didn't want to be the recipient of others' sympathies—it was hard and shameful to me. I also learned along the way that, for me, the more I talked about the situation the less I prayed. Talking about it was so draining that I didn't even want to talk to God. For me, the best way to handle it was to keep it to myself and very few praying friends."

NEED TO KNOW SIX: Your family will experience the ultimate test of your core values: Will you live according to what you say you believe?

Randy and Alicia had always supported the local women's pregnancy resource center—both by volunteering and giving financially. They had always been vocal about their principles concerning the value of life, unconditional love, and commitment to their family. However, in their eighteen-year-old marriage those core values had not been deeply challenged until they learned of their sixteen-year-old daughter's unplanned pregnancy.

According to Miami Valley (OH) Women's Center executive director, Linda Schindler, when a young woman is ambivalent about her decision to abort or to carry the child to term, her parents tend to express their support of whatever decision she plans to make. However, when the young woman clearly chooses life, parental support, in some cases, disappears. How could that be?

"What this pregnancy feels like to parents in the initial stages," Linda explained, "can be stated in one word—threat."[2] What is threatened for parents?

- Their reputation is threatened.
- Their way of life is threatened.
- Their parenting skills are threatened.
- Their plans for their own future are threatened.
- Their family system, as they have known it, is threatened.

What do people usually do when threatened? They have a "fight or flight" response. Often, even in the minds of parents whose core values scream pro-life, abortion offers a way to "get rid of the threat." They can flee reality and "no one would know." Initially, this can look like an easy way out of the whole threatening situation.

Katie's mom, Jill, said that her daughter's pregnancy made her feel like the world she had known was now invaded by this overwhelming situation.

"I didn't see the baby as a baby in those early weeks," Jill explained. "I saw 'this problem' as a threat to my competency as a parent. This problem shadowed me everywhere I went. A haunting question nagged at me: What would people say if they knew? I not only saw 'this problem' as a threat to me, but to Katie as well. I mentioned abortion to her, stating that it would allow her to finish school. I was convinced she wasn't ready to be a mom, and the birth father—well, I didn't even like him. I cannot believe now, looking at our precious five-year-old grandson, that I catered to thoughts of abortion even for one moment."

Jill and her family are not the only ones who visited the possibility of abortion. In chapter 4, we will be discussing the abortion decision as it impacts all who are touched by it.

NEED TO KNOW SEVEN: You have the gift of time. God will make a way.
When parents face these life-changing circumstances, it is important they know that answers will come as they give God time. Parents who walked this rough and rocky path confirm the truth that God does make a way.

brenda

One of the major truths God taught me is this: He is the Creator. He created baby Jenna (even though the circumstances were not His will). He loved her and has a special plan for her, as well as for my daughter. I am to feel the same for this creation. I am to trust Him and know that all is well. When we walked through those dark valleys, He was there. He understood our trials and grief. He continues to this day to work out all things for our good.

keith

This wasn't where we were supposed to be as a family. This type of thing only happened in other families. However, as the reality set in for us, we realized just how much our son needed us to walk this with him—not in anger, but with understanding. I learned that my son needed me to model what a godly and mature response looked like, and God enabled me to do that.

trudy

When our daughter ran away and had been gone for almost seven weeks, we prayed for her continually. When Annie did call us to let us know she was safe, we were ecstatic. She was coming home, and we would put her in a drug detox program immediately. That was when we found out that she was pregnant.

Before all this happened with Annie, I guess you might consider me a "fair-weather Christian." Now I am very different. I had always believed in God, but I just didn't have time for Him in my life. Now I am so thankful for everything that has happened. I've learned that I cannot fix or straighten anything out unless I am doing God's will. He is the only one who can make things right. God gives me strength and power that I never experienced until I went through what we did with our daughter.

God's will is not always easy, but it is always right. We knew that we could not provide for Annie's baby and that she was not in any position to do so either. God enabled us to find the proper people to talk with in making our decision to plan an adoption for this little one. I have learned that I can always trust God with any problem, for He will make a way. My God is an awesome God, and I love Him with all my heart.

IN SUMMARY

As parents move through the initial days of a daughter's or son's unplanned pregnancy, there are seven things they need to know:

- Parents will experience myriad painful and confusing emotions.
- Your daughter or son is journeying to a place where she or he has never been. Your response and support are critical.
- Fathers and mothers may deal with this family crisis in totally

different ways, potentially leaving one parent feeling alone and unsupported.

- Parents will need to find a balance between supporting their young adult and letting her take responsibility.
- Parents and their child will need to decide who, when, and how to tell family and friends.
- Your family will experience the ultimate test of your core values: Will you live according to what you say you believe?
- You have the gift of time. God will make a way.

questions for REFLECTION and DISCUSSION

1. How did you learn of your daughter's pregnancy? Or how did you learn that your son was going to be a father?
2. How has this impacted your relationship with your young adult?
3. How has this impacted how you see yourself as a parent?
4. What major issues are you struggling with?
5. What decisions need to be made now? Later?

your son, the pregnancy, and you

3

KEY ISSUES PATERNAL BIRTH GRANDPARENTS MUST FACE

> Our son is going to be a father. That just can't be. It seems like yesterday we were watching his Little League game. Our son is going to be a father. I am still stunned about all of this. Where do we go from here? Who can we talk to?
>
> MARSHA, JAKE'S MOM

HOW DID KEN and Susan hear? Rick, their son, slipped a note under their bedroom door as he left earlier than usual for first period at his high school. It was a short note, right to the point. Rick was always that way. It simply read, *"A week ago, Rebecca told me she is pregnant. I know that we have really messed things up. I don't know what we are going to do about it yet. I am sorry, Rick."*

How did Emily, a single mom, hear? When she got home from work that eventful evening, there was a phone message from Karen, her son's girlfriend's mother. *"Emily, please call me right away,"* she said. *"We have a major problem. Jennifer is pregnant, at least two months. We need to talk, tonight!"*

How did Roger and Cindy hear? Cindy was sitting in the car waiting to pick up her sixteen-year-old daughter from volleyball practice. Rachel came running out, tear-stained and angry. *"You know what they are saying at school? Kelly is pregnant and my brother is the father. How can I face anyone again?"*

It's no accident that parents often hear indirectly of their son's involvement in an unplanned pregnancy. Not only is the news just as devastating for these parents as it is for the parents of the expectant mother, but the

53

journey is uncharted territory full of uncertainty.

According to Mary Martin Mason, author of *Out of the Shadows: Birthfathers' Stories,* young fathers have difficulty coming to terms with the fact that they are going to be dads and even greater difficulty informing their parents. "I have heard of any number of ways that parents are informed, but more often than not it is not from their son, but from the young woman who is pregnant and/or her family. Unlike motherhood, fatherhood can be evaded, covered up, and denied. While the public generally takes the attitude that birth fathers in unplanned pregnancies have an easy time of it, reality is that they are at risk for denying the impact of this experience."[1] And the impact on birth fathers, as on birth mothers, is weighty and lifelong.

In attempting to examine the concerns and needs of young men and their families in an unplanned pregnancy, I discovered a major gap in research literature and resources. There is little written to support these families as they move through this life-altering crisis. This chapter seeks to provide insight into the key issues faced by the father and his parents.

ISSUE ONE: *The cultural perception of men and their role in an unplanned pregnancy has a profound impact on young unwed fathers.*

Over a decade ago a major survey of adoption agencies measured the involvement of fathers in the adoption process. The survey asked the question: Who is your client? A number of them named birth mothers. A number of them named the child. "Expectant and birth fathers were most at risk of being overlooked and underserved as clients."[2]

According to John Ensor, director of A Women's Concern in Boston, Massachusetts, numerous pregnancy resource centers and adoption agencies have been seeking ways to reach young fathers, but for decades this didn't happen. "Most centers are directed by women and see mostly women," Ensor commented.[3] "It has been our default mode, not purposely intended." Until recently, the important role and responsibility of a young father in the decision-making process has been left unaddressed. Why is that?

Jim Pye, director of the Men's Ministry, Hope Pregnancy Centers of Brazos Valley, Texas, since 2000, says, "We are living in a culture that for the last thirty or forty years has progressively degraded maleness. Out of the feminist movement came the cry, 'We don't need men.' There has been a subtle cultural erosion of how a man sees himself and his position in the family structure."[4] If, according to the feminist ideology, men are generally not needed, their involvement within the context of an unplanned pregnancy is often considered completely unwelcome. However, this doesn't hold true for all young women who are pregnant. Many do want the fathers of their babies to be present and involved.

Another reason why men have been excluded from consideration comes out of *Roe v. Wade*, explains Pye. It has to do with how men are viewed in relationship to their paternal rights.

> *Roe v. Wade* has had a profound effect on the role of fathers and the common perception of fatherhood. Cunning, persuasive phrases, such as 'reproductive choice' and 'a woman's right to choose,' have obfuscated the fact that the rights of the father have been abrogated by legal decree. This denial of the father's rights to protect his child lies at the core of the erosion of fatherhood.[5]

If a father wants to parent, to take steps to protect and provide for his baby, he has no legal recourse in attempting to save that baby's life. He is powerless.

Pye asserts that another thing *Roe v. Wade* has done to further destroy the role of a father in an unplanned pregnancy is that it has fostered irresponsibility in men. It provides what is perceived as a quick fix to the "problem," and the ability of the father to just walk away.

In unplanned pregnancies, says Mary Martin Mason, "public sentiment, media, and common attitudes blame the father. Young men in this circumstance are treated as young unwed mothers were twenty or thirty years ago—shamed and excluded from the decision-making process. Today a birth mother making a plan for adoption is encouraged to connect to the child she is relinquishing in order to psychologically say good-bye. Birth fathers in these same circumstances are, in many cases, given little support or education regarding how to grieve this profound loss."[6]

A number of studies examining young unmarried parents in recent years have focused almost exclusively on mothers. Not until the past five years or so has there been any consideration of the needs and concerns of young unwed fathers. A study done by Newcastle University looked at a group of single, nonresidential, noncustodial fathers aged 16–24 in order to assess their needs, concerns, and desires.[7] Two concerns highlighted by the study were:

- Fathers said they were made to feel unimportant both during the pregnancy and after the birth. Little effort was made to encourage them to develop and maintain involvement with their child.
- Few young men were aware of their lack of legal rights in relation to their child. There was misinformation both among fathers and those working with them. No information on rights was readily available to them.

Unwed fathers are particularly unlikely to stay connected to their children over time, says Wade Horn, editor of *The Fatherhood Movement: A Call to Action*. During the first two years of their child's life, 57 percent of unwed fathers visit their child at least once per week; but by the time their child reaches seven and one-half years old, that percentage drops to less than 25 percent.[8]

When an unmarried father is not living with his child's mother at the time of birth, he is very unlikely to stay involved in his child's life over the long term, adds Horn. If the noncustodial father marries someone other than the child's mother, he is especially unlikely to remain in contact with his children.[9]

The lack of rights and services available to a young father and his family hinges on myths widely believed by the public and practiced by social services agencies.

ISSUE TWO: Negative myths about young unwed fathers perpetuate a lack of paternal involvement.

"Loser," "irresponsible," or "uncaring" are words commonly used to describe a father in an unplanned pregnancy. According to Brenda Romanchik, director of Insight: Open Adoption Resources and Support, in Royal Oak, Michigan, not only is it often assumed that an unwed father doesn't care about his unborn child, but he is considered the adversary by the girl's family.[10] The picture for many young men is no different than it was thirty or forty years ago when at figurative "gunpoint" the birth father was ordered to stay away. No contact. No involvement. No future with the child or mother.

In addition to the myth that a young man glories in the pregnancy as proof of his machismo is the assumption that most young birth fathers are more concerned about themselves than their partner or the child and are unwilling to support them. According to Jim Pye, the public may be surprised at how many of these men are willing to accept responsibility and do their best to provide in spite of great economic hardships.

"Many people say teen dads don't care for their children," says author and researcher Archie Wortham. "They think that teen dads only want to make girls pregnant. While that may be true of some, it's not true of most. And though many teen dads know they've made a mistake, they still get up each day and try anyway to do the right thing. They try to make a family, with or without the help of the baby's grandparents."[11] This includes a young man's own parents, who in some cases resist helping him make responsible decisions about the future.

A third myth about young unwed fathers is that they are not impacted by an abortion and suffer no harm from the experience. The truth is, young men, whether they are a party to the abortion decision or it happens without their prior knowledge or approval, are at high risk for future psychological and relational problems.

In his thought-provoking article about "forgotten fathers" and their unforgettable children, Dr. David Reardon, director of the Elliot Institute in Springfield, Illinois, writes:

In the early seventies, Arthur Shostak accompanied his lover to a well-groomed suburban abortion clinic. They had both agreed abortion was best. But sitting in the waiting room proved to be a "bruising experience." By the time he left the clinic, he was shocked by how deeply disturbed he had become.

A professor of sociology at Drexel University in Philadelphia, Shostak spent the subsequent ten years studying the abortion experience of men. His study included a survey of 1,000 men who accompanied wives or girlfriends to abortion clinics.[12]

Shostak's study found that abortion is far more stressful for men than the public would generally suppose. More than one in four equated abortion to murder. Slightly over 80% said they had already begun to think about the child that might have been born (with 29% saying they had been fantasizing about the child "frequently"), 68% believed men involved in abortions "did not have an easy time of it," and 47% worried about having disturbing thoughts afterwards. Shostak reported that many men began to cry during the interview. . . . Many expressed frustration and anger about the failure of women to consider their wishes and feelings. They felt isolated from the decision and—especially if they opposed the abortion—emasculated and powerless.

In a subsequent interview Shostak said: "Most of the men I talk to think about the abortion years after it is over. They feel sad, they feel curious, they feel a lot of things; but usually they have talked to no one about it. It's a taboo. . . . With a man, if he wants to shed a tear, he had better do it privately. If he feels that the abortion had denied him his child, he had better work through it himself. He does not share his pain with a clergyman, a minister; he does not share it with a close male friend. . . . It just stays with him. And it stays for a long time."[13]

Men have reported a large number of problems that they claim were a direct result of their abortion experience. These include broken relationships, sexual dysfunction, substance abuse, self-hate, risk taking and suicidal behavior, increasing feelings of grief over time, feelings of helplessness, guilt, depression, greater tendencies toward becoming angry and violent, and feelings connected to a sense of lost manhood.[14]

According to Dr. Vincent Rue, one of the nation's most experienced psychologists in the field of post-abortion issues, "Induced abortion reinforces defective problem solving on the part of the male by encouraging detachment, desertion, and irresponsibility. . . . Abortion rewrites the rules of masculinity. While a male is expected to be strong, abortion makes him feel weak. A male is expected to be responsible, yet abortion encourages him to act without concern for the innocent and to destroy any identifiable and undesirable outcomes of his sexual decision making and/or attachments. . . . Whether or not the male was involved in the abortion decision, his inability to function in a socially prescribed manner (i.e., to protect and provide) leaves him wounded and confused."[15]

ISSUE THREE: Birth fathers and their families are often left out of crucial decision making.

"Once they hear that their son is going to be a father," says Brenda Romanchik, "a big worry for them is 'Will we be invited to the table?' Often birth fathers' families are also considered the enemy along with their sons, and especially if the paternal grandparents want to help and assist. The message they often receive during this crisis time is that 'you are the outsider' in this process and it is best that it stays that way."[16]

The truth is that the paternal grandparents are as much grandparents to the unborn child as the maternal grandparents are. According to John Ensor, the main issue for young men and their families that makes the entire experience different for them is that they have absolutely no control. "A great worry for the parents of the young man involves the answer to one question: 'What are they (our son and his girlfriend) going to do?' Some parents won't 'humanize' the child in their thinking because they want an abortion."[17]

Other times, the opposite is true. Jim Pye says, "If the young lady is abortion minded, the boy's family frantically asks, 'How can we influence this decision? What can we do to save the life of our grandchild? How can we help this young girl?' The painful, stark, devastating reality is: If she wants an abortion, there is nothing they can do."[18] Neither birth fathers nor their families have any legal recourse.

There are a number of options that young unwed men can choose—

none of which the grandparents have any say over, and clearly no power. Those options, Ensor explains, are:

- *He never tells.*

Of course, with this option, the parents are uninformed and are not "worrying" about the crisis. There are many young man who have hidden the pregnancy problem from their parents, and the parents never learn the truth until years later. This secrecy brings only postponed devastation and pain to the family because, in many cases, the choice made was abortion.

- *She chooses to have the baby; the young man is pushing for abortion.*

He may turn to his parents in hopes of gaining support for what he wants to happen. He hopes that by pulling them into the decision they can apply the pressure needed to convince her to terminate the pregnancy.

- *She chooses abortion; he wants to parent the child.*

The mother of the child is in complete control. Young men have no legal standing in the abortion decision. When it happens the devastated young man is left grieving and broken. What makes it even more grievous for young men is her "right of privacy" becomes his sentence of silence. He is bombarded with emotions of grief, anger, and guilt . . . and no one can know the cause.

"A number of years ago," Ensor continued, "a pastor contacted me to tell me about his son. His girlfriend was pregnant and planning an abortion. The young man and his family were deeply committed to doing the right thing. All of their efforts to intervene in the girl's and family's decision were ignored and the abortion happened. The anguish all had to be worked out in silence. They were powerless to help their son or grandbaby. The devastation and torment was long-term for all. Of course, not only was the baby aborted, but also the relationship of this young couple."[19]

- *She and her family choose adoption; the boy and his family disagree.*

"In the fall of 1998, my husband died," Cheryl said. "He had a heart attack while working in the lawn. He just fell over and was immediately gone at the age of fifty. Just before my husband's death, Jonathan, our 'prodigal son,' informed us about his girlfriend's pregnancy.

"Adoption was not an option for us at that point. I had worked at crisis pregnancy centers with girls, sharing with them that the adoption option was a positive choice. Now, here I was faced with it, and I didn't want to make it. I thought my son and his girlfriend would reconcile. Margie was bitter about the pregnancy and shut him out of her life.

"We got a phone call one afternoon from the adoption agency, and they wanted us to come in for a meeting. By that time, I was facing this as a widow of only a brief time. This was the first Jonathan and I knew that Margie and her parents had been to an adoption agency. It turned out that they had been working with this agency for almost three months. They had already picked out the family they wanted. It was a total shock to us . . . and we were still hoping for reconciliation; I had great hopes of being able to watch my grandson grow up.

"We went for the meeting and were sitting there that day with the counselor at the adoption agency. She was young . . . unseasoned in her work. She matter of factly said to us that the decision had been made. This is what they wanted, and they just needed my son to sign the papers that it was fine with us, too. It wasn't that simple for me. I burst into tears. I am not a crier, but this was such a broadside.

"I said to this young adoption worker, 'Do you realize what you are asking us to do? He has an incredible heritage, this little boy, and he will never know it.' I was torn apart thinking that we were going to give him away.

"We said we would go home and pray. My prayer was that Jonathan and Margie would either reconcile or that we would accept that we would have to be open to adoption. Over a matter of weeks and through a number of circumstances, the Lord made it clear that adoption was the best choice for this little one. We met the adoptive family and just knew that they were perfect for our little fellow. We know where he is, and we will be able to watch him grow up from afar. Both my heart and my son's are at peace."

- *Together they choose adoption and work positively toward that end.*

When Kyle and Katie, both seventeen, learned that she was pregnant, Kyle went to his parents broken and frightened. After the initial shock, Kyle's father worked with him on accepting responsibility for his behavior. Kyle and his family scheduled a family meeting with Katie and her parents. Although emotions were strained and tense initially, as the evening progressed the families were able to talk openly with each other. Over the course of the following months, both families and Kyle and Katie made the decision that this little one needed to grow up in a two-parent home where the adults were mature and ready to parent. Kyle and Katie both agreed that being part of the decision making regarding the selection of the adoptive family would be important for all concerned, including their parents. The young couple selected the adoptive family, both families met them, and all were present at Michael's birth.

ISSUE FOUR: Both birth fathers and their families face unique emotional and practical challenges in the midst of an unplanned pregnancy.

"When a parent hears of the pregnancy which involves their son, within two and a half seconds, their world is spinning," says John Ensor.[20] "Much like the experience for the girl's parents, it feels like a 'psychic' death. With the words, 'she's pregnant,' there comes a death to the life they have projected for him . . . going to college, finding a sweet girl, getting married, and then baby . . . all in order. The pregnancy brings that all to a screeching halt in their hearts and minds."

Jim Pye agrees. "Depending on the social-economic status of the family, parents will have different worries. If their son is in high school, headed for college, or is in college, they fear for his future, his goals. 'Has he shipwrecked those goals we had for him?' If the family is from a lower social-economic position, the worry might be how their son will be able to support the needs of the baby and the baby's mother."[21]

"Parents," adds Mary Martin Mason, "worry about the crisis that surrounds the unplanned pregnancy and the outcome for their son, for the mother, for the child, as well as for themselves. The pregnancy and pending birth create an automatic lifetime connection for their son with a young woman who is pregnant. No matter what happens with the child, through that child they have created a link to one another that will continue to play out in their futures, impacting their marriages, births of other children (who will be half-sibs to this child), extended family, and so on. I have noticed that as paternal grandparents begin to grasp the reality of this, they may try to counsel, interfere, protect, and take on all the parenting roles that emerge when a mom or dad perceives their child is in crisis.

"Young men in the midst of an unplanned pregnancy," Mason continues, "tend to react in typical ways to this crisis. They have been programmed to deny the profundity of the experience, to demonstrate their feelings in physical or demonstrative ways. They may show anger. They may respond in total denial and flee. Both anger and denial mask profound fear and profound loss at the possibility that they will be blamed, discounted, and ultimately, excluded."[22]

Romanchik agrees. "He may become angry and withdraw out of a sense of failure. He may feel an overwhelming sense of an inability to provide for this child. He may feel that he just can't do it. This will cause him to control whatever he can, often through anger, or simply by giving up and disappearing."[23]

"A young father has difficulty in really feeling connected to the pregnancy," commented Carrie Fiasco, adoption manager at the Children's Home of Cincinnati, Ohio. "In my work as a pregnancy counselor, I found that they did not participate in counseling as much. It was easier for them to disconnect from what was happening because they were not experiencing the physical changes. It really wasn't a pregnancy to them. Until they saw a clear ultrasound or until the actual birth of the baby, they did not recognize themselves as a father, and it was much easier for them to be in denial."[24]

It is not uncommon to hear a young father continue to refer to the child as "it," even after the gender is known. By depersonalizing the child, the young man is expressing what he is feeling—a physical and emotional distance between him and his soon-to-be-born child.

With the emotional turmoil swirling around their son, families face challenges that, left unrecognized and unaddressed, can have hurtful, long-term consequences.

- *Communicating with the young woman and her family.*

"Perhaps the greatest challenge facing the young man and his family is communicating with the parents of his girlfriend," says John Ensor. "It is imperative for a healthy outcome to the situation for the young people and both sets of parents to pull together in working through the difficult issues that confront them. Otherwise, it is 'war' everywhere.

"I tell families that pregnancy is not cancer—it is not death. As soon as families can, they need to begin talking. I also tell the young man's family that it is his responsibility to begin the dialogue (with their support if needed).[25]

- *Giving your son the right message.*

Yes, parents are deeply disappointed in most cases when a pregnancy occurs as the result of their son's behavior. The message that follows the disclosure can be key in guiding the young man through positive and right decisions.

Archie Wortham, in his article, *Teen Fathers Need a Dad, Too!*, writes:

The pregnancy happened and the adult thing to do is handle it with a degree of parental understanding these young parents need, rather than lecture and ostracize as some of us are predisposed to do. What really makes these teen fathers different from teen dads of the past is economics. In 1970, a young boy could get a job, and actually had hopes of making things work. But since 1973, the median weekly earning for teenagers dropped 30%, but for males 25 and older, the drop was only 7%. Translation—some of us older dads really need to examine how we might treat a potential father of our grandchildren—it's tough for them! We need to look them in the eye and challenge them to show responsibility and courage. Emphasizing they should get involved in the baby's life might be a better tact to use in communicating the importance of fatherhood, rather than holding a shotgun at eye level and telling them they're worthless and you never want to see them again. This loving but firm parental approach with compassionate understanding for the young child might make them feel part of a family. . . .

If a baby has resulted from their irresponsibility of trying to be an adult, then it's the real adults around the baby who have the responsibility to make sure the baby's life is not hampered by misguided guilt, misunderstanding, or refusal to accept the fact. If it were one of my sons who were that irresponsible, I'd try to reach beyond the shame, mortification, and desire to carve them up as embarrassments. I'd try to shoulder some of the responsibility by trying to understand how I could possibly keep from making matters worse.

Accepting the situation doesn't condone the action. Rather than harping on how I went wrong, or how bad a parent I might feel, I'd fulfill the role of a "grown up" by concentrating on what is best for those involved. I'd concentrate on helping them help themselves and be careful I didn't assume too much responsibility. It's their job to baby-sit. It's their job to continue school. It's their job to take care of their child. It's my job to love them, love their baby, and find enough love to keep from feeling devastated for one mistake. We all make mistakes. It's when people continue to remind us of our mistakes that we stop wanting to get up in the morning.[26]

- *Expecting too little from your son.*

"The need to provide for his child is huge for a birth father," says Mary Martin Mason. "In this field, we have far too long left the birth father out of the decision-making process. I feel you get what you expect. If you expect him not to be there, not to participate, then that is exactly what you will get. It is so much better to get him involved—for the sake of the child and for himself."[27]

Part of that involvement begins with a first step, offers Jim Pye. "It is a healthy expectation to guide the young man in accepting responsibility and consequences of his actions. He needs to know that the expectations for him are to be responsible to the child . . . to value, honor, and cherish life.

The hope from you as his parents is that you will support him in a decision to choose life."[28]

Another expectation for the young man has to do with restoration, Pye adds. "In working with young men, I tell them, 'You have dishonored this girl and broken God's commandments. It is important to confess this sin and ask forgiveness of her, her parents, and of God.'"[29]

• *Helping your son through grief and loss.*

If abortion or adoption is chosen for a young man's child, the paternal grandparents will need to step up to the plate and offer support, even when they are hurting themselves. "For a person to help another through grief and loss," says Pye, "sacrifice is called for. As parents, whenever we enter into the broken lives of our children, it will be disruptive and it is going to cost us—physically and emotionally. Extending our hands and hearts to support our sons emotionally, spiritually, and practically as they move through their confusion and fear to restoration isn't easy. But parents just can't keep up the daily routine as though nothing has happened. It is voluntary suffering to step into the pain of another in order to open their heart to God's healing and restoration."[30]

ISSUE FIVE: *Parents can play a vital role in supporting and guiding their son through the most important event in his life: becoming a father.*
An unplanned pregnancy can be the single most significant turning point in a boy's journey to becoming a man. As he is propelled into maturity and responsibility, his role as a man is clarified and tested.

"God created the role of a man to fulfill His perfect design," says John Ensor. "The first role man was given was to be protector. God's design for man in the family was to protect his family, to be the spiritual head, and to be the gatekeeper. When a man advocates for an abortion, or walks away from his pregnant girlfriend, he abdicates his role as protector. When he embraces the unexpected challenges of fatherhood, on the other hand, he quickly 'grows up.' His call to be a protector of his child leads him to make all kinds of new commitments."[31]

The second God-given mandate for a man is to provide for the well-being of his children. What is he to provide? A father is to provide safety, love, and nurturance. Every child, from the moment of conception, has been entrusted into the care of his or her father. When a man takes on the role of father, "he finds new energy to work, to sacrifice, and to make other mature decisions because he wants to be a provider," Ensor affirmed.

"Parents need to know and to help their son deal with the reality that he is already a father—NOW," says Pye. "He has responsibilities—NOW, not in nine months—to provide for and protect his child and the baby's mother."

Parents also need to know that their son will be dealing with fear, shame, and anger, adds Pye. "Men have a God-given instinct to protect and provide. As this instinct kicks in, it may result in anger due to the inability to do what he feels he should. One essential thing parents can do is to nurture their son's fathering instinct. Sometimes that means he will marry his girlfriend and be actively parenting. Sometimes this means that although they do not marry, he can play a key role in his child's life. And, sometimes this doesn't mean that he will be parenting his child. Adoption is a wonderful option to help a young birth father meet his goals of providing the best for his child."[32]

IN SUMMARY

A young man involved in an unplanned pregnancy and his family have the following issues to face:

- The cultural perception of men and their role in an unplanned pregnancy has a profound impact on young unwed fathers.
- Negative myths about young unwed fathers perpetuate a lack of paternal involvement.
- Birth fathers and their families are often left out of crucial decision making.
- Both birth fathers and their families face unique emotional and practical challenges in the midst of an unplanned pregnancy.

• Parents can play a vital role in supporting and guiding their son through the most important event in his life: becoming a father.

In maneuvering through these issues, it is important to remember the following:

• It is essential to communicate with the young woman and her family.
• It is crucial to give our sons the right message.
• It is important to have healthy expectation for our sons.
• It is necessary to be prepared to help our sons through grief and loss if abortion or adoption occurs.
• It is healing and restorative to help our sons understand their role as a father.

questions for REFLECTION and DISCUSSION

1. How did you learn about your son's involvement in an unplanned pregnancy?
2. What part have you played in the decision-making process?
3. What are the barriers you have encountered in having a voice regarding the pregnancy?
4. What have been your greatest concerns about your son? Yourself?
5. What was the outcome of the pregnancy? Abortion, adoption, parenting? How do you feel about the decision? How are you dealing with the decision?

part two

critical
decisions

the grandchild you may never know

4

THE LONG-TERM IMPACT OF ABORTION ON THE FAMILY

> Numb is perhaps the only word that truly describes how we felt when our daughter told us of her pregnancy. There was only one answer for us, we thought. After all, she was only sixteen. Really, what other option did we have?
>
> DEBORAH, JENN'S MOM

THEY DIDN'T KNOW I knew. But I did. I knew that their eighteen-year-old daughter was pregnant. I had been the pastor at their church for several years. The twenty-year-old father of the baby had been in to see me. He was devastated and broken. He told me her parents didn't know that she was pregnant, and she had planned an abortion. He didn't know when for sure, just soon.

They didn't know I knew. But I did. I don't think *they* knew . . . yet. But I saw it in her eyes. She and her father walked in and sat down in the fifth pew from the front of the church. It was just ten days after the young man had come to me. I knew that she had experienced the abortion. Her once sparkling eyes were dark and sad. She sat remote, just staring ahead. Her father reached over to put his arm around her, but she brushed it away. In that moment, I feared that she would begin to push much more than that away.

They didn't know I knew. But I did. I heard it in the father's panicked voice. When I picked up the call, he spoke just above a whisper. "Can you help us? My daughter needs counseling." His voice faded away as if by a grief-stricken thought.

"What's the problem?" I asked.

"Well," he stammered, "my daughter is just real depressed. We found a note tonight in her room. She had started it and then left with a friend."

The man sounded desperate. In his voice I could detect incredible fear and worst of all helplessness. "The note was written to God," he said. "She told God that there was no point in living any longer."

His tone changed from that hushed whisper to gasps of grief. "I love her so much, but we're losing her." He was silent for a moment, then he pleaded, "Please, can you do something?"

I asked this father if anything else had happened with his daughter in recent days that would precipitate this suicidal note.

He hesitated. Silence, and then . . . "Well, Kim *was* pregnant. We just found out . . . " His words stopped with a gasp.

"Did your daughter have an abortion?" I asked. It was out. The word was said: *abortion*. Again, there was silence followed by a tidal wave of weeping.

I met Kim the next Saturday in my office. She agreed to come if her parents didn't have to be there. She began to relate the details that led up to the abortion. Never making eye contact with me, she said, "My dad and mom didn't know I was pregnant. I just couldn't tell them and disappoint them. My friends at school talked me into an abortion. They convinced me that it was the only option. My parents had already made plans for me to go to college, the one they had both gone to. Having a baby right now would put an end to those plans for me. I couldn't do that to them. But what I have done . . . " She suddenly couldn't talk for the tears. She buried her head in her lap.

Kim, like thousands of young women each year, faced an untimely pregnancy. The question— *What will I do?*—propels many young women to choose abortion. Some parents don't know about the pregnancy, yet others do, and for them the question is the same— *What will we will do?* For over a quarter of a million Christian young women, men, and their families each year, that choice is abortion.[1,2]

why would your daughter choose abortion?

When a young woman looks at the positive pregnancy test results, she also sees her future rapidly slipping away. What perhaps were plans for college after high school or a bright career after college are potentially wiped away by the looming "threat." In the initial stages, when knowledge of the pregnancy is limited to a few confidants, a young woman begins her fantasy of flight— *What can I do to take care of this problem?* She usually is not thinking "baby," nor is she thinking long-term about any other areas of life that might be touched by her decision.

Research regarding the abortion decision indicates that most thoughts fall under the umbrella word *threat.*[3] A pregnancy at an inopportune time represents many threats, such as:

- Threat of the loss of a future college education
- Threat of rejection by parents or boyfriend
- Threat of financial insecurity
- Threat of the loss of a lifestyle she has known
- Threat of the loss of respect and reputation if the pregnancy was known

In looking beyond the obvious losses that are a part of an unplanned pregnancy, Dr. Charles Kenny, president of Kenny & Associates, Inc. (also known as *The Right Brain People*®) conducted research directed at the questions surrounding a woman's feelings about abortion and how that perception relates to other options, such as parenting or adoption. Young women experiencing an unplanned pregnancy perceive the pregnancy and having a child as an experience that forever changes them, Dr. Kenny says. They feel that their core identity—who they are and want to be—is now out of their control. "Such a radical change in who they believe themselves to be," says Dr. Kenny, "is the emotional equivalent of death. So strong is the fear of death of the familiar self that abortion is seen by these women as a means of self-preservation. Even though these women believe abortion is wrong—

that it is evil—they also recognize it as something that will prevent the death of the self, which, to them, is an even greater evil. So, the decision to abort is not a direct decision, but rather is arrived at almost by default as an act of self-preservation."[4]

Why don't these women consider making an adoption plan for their unplanned child? According to Dr. Kenny, "They dismiss adoption as an alternative very early in the process of thinking through their options. To them it provides no resolution to their dilemma." In fact, Dr. Kenny contends, "It is a loathsome act because of their professed assumption that the adopted child would be abused or neglected. And they think any child 'given up' for adoption would feel rejected, unloved, or abandoned." Abandoning one's own child to strangers is perceived as tantamount to "throwing the child to the wolves."

Dr. Kenny also learned that for these women, adoption creates an irresolvable spiritual conflict because in their minds, "adoption means two deaths—the death of the child by abandonment and the death of the self by carrying the child to term." Adoption is actually perceived as a greater evil than abortion.

In his article, "Abortion: A Failure to Communicate," which is based on Dr. Kenny's research, Paul Swope cites a study titled "Abortion, the Least of Three Evils—Understanding the Psychological Dynamics of How Women Feel About Abortion." In discussing that study, Swope suggests women do not see any "good" that can come from an untimely pregnancy. "Instead," he says, "they must weigh what they perceive as three 'evils'—namely motherhood, adoption, and abortion."[5] Unplanned motherhood, according to the study, represents a threat so great to modern women that it is perceived as equivalent to a death to self. "While the woman may rationally understand this is not her own literal death, her emotional subconscious reaction to carrying the child to term is that her life will be over."[6]

How is that so? Young women of today, Swope points out, have developed an identity that simply does not include early motherhood. Thoughts of finishing school, getting a good job, even getting married are considered positive; but motherhood is not for now. When an unplanned pregnancy invades a woman's life, she perceives it as a loss of "her present and future self. It shatters her sense of who she is and will become. It paralyses her ability to think rationally."[7]

When a young woman faces an unplanned pregnancy, she does not ask herself, "Is this a baby?" Rather, in those early weeks and months, she asks herself, "How can I preserve my own life?" Abortion becomes her only answer.

why would your son choose abortion?

Young men who are faced with untimely pregnancy also face serious questions. Many of them choose abortion for the same reasons that a young woman does. It is a threat to them as well. According to Warren Williams, a counselor who specializes in ministry to men, young men become involved in an abortion in one of five ways: (1) they encourage or support the woman to choose abortion; (2) they pressure her to abort; (3) they abandon her to make the decision alone; (4) they unsuccessfully oppose the abortion; or (5) they learn about the abortion only after it has been done.[8]

"Most young men," says Jim Pye, director of the Men's Ministry with Hope Pregnancy Center in Brazos Valley, Texas, "harbor the erroneous belief that they *will* be a father in nine months if something is not done to change the situation."[9] Because he does not see himself as a father *now*, the abortion-minded man does not believe he is aborting his own fatherhood, only avoiding it. Conversely, Pye comments, "He believes he has nothing to lose because he does not bear the physical burden of the pregnancy nor does he have to endure to procedure." What these men fail to grasp is that they are fathers already with the responsibility to enter into a relationship with their preborn child through the support, protection, and care of the child's mother.

why do grandparents choose abortion?

"One of the many heartbreaking experiences I have had over the years," said one pregnancy resource center director, "was the afternoon a minister walked into our clinic with his teenage daughter. At that time our center was located next to an abortion mill and he thought that was where he was.

When he realized that abortion was something we didn't do, he didn't stay, but went next door."

Catherine Hickem, L.C.S.W., psychotherapist and founder of the mother/daughter ministry Kingdom Princess Ministries in south Florida, regularly counsels post-abortive women. She began to pay particular attention to the question, "What influences a young woman's decision to have an abortion?" What she discovered disheartened her. "In women's decisions to get abortions, there is an interesting theme that surfaces in the decision-making process—their mothers."[10]

Why would a Christian mother push her daughter to have an abortion? The post-abortive women Hickem counsels indicated that the number-one reason they had an abortion was "their mothers' belief that having this baby would ruin their lives. These young, frightened, hurting young women were told two things over and over again—that they would never have the life they had dreamed of and that their mothers would not be around to help raise this child."[11]

One reason mothers give this message, says Hickem, is simply selfishness. Sadly, and too late, these Christian mothers wake up to the fact that their response to their daughter's pregnancy was more about them than their daughter—and certainly not about their unborn grandchild.

Shame is another reason some mothers push for abortion. "Guilt is feeling bad about what you have done, and shame is feeling bad about who you are. When a person experiences shame, it becomes a powerful force that overshadows every other internal characteristic. It is an extremely damaging and painful emotion. A mother can experience a sense of failure when her daughter finds herself in an out-of-wedlock pregnancy. This is especially true for Christian women. This feeling manifests itself as shame in the mother's heart. She looks at the pregnancy as a personal affront from the daughter, and there now will be a public display of her failure to teach her daughter morality."[12]

Driven by fear of being rejected by their mothers, some young women follow the stern advice even if they do not agree with it. Hickem writes, "I can't tell you how many times I've heard a woman say to me, 'I didn't want the abortion, and I knew it was wrong. But I went through with it anyway because I just couldn't bear the thought of my mother holding it against me all of my life.' These post-abortive women honestly believed if they got rid of the baby, they would regain their mother's blessing. The tragedy that comes to many is that their mothers never forget their 'mistake' and are quick to question their judgment in all the other areas of their life from then on. Trust rarely returns between them." Sadly, if the maternal blessing was lost because of the pregnancy, the young woman probably never had it in the first place.

What about fathers? What is their role in the abortion decision?

"Sadly, in most cases, we don't see the fathers," Hickem says. "It really depends on the structure of the family—how the family system operates." If the family is led by a strong, authoritarian father, who needs to always be right, his daughter may never tell either parent of the pregnancy. She has learned two things while growing up: that there is no "wiggle room" for mistakes as far as her father is concerned, and that her mother is too weak to be supportive of her. The result is an abortion that only one person in the family knows about.

On the flip side of the authoritarian father is the passive father. In this family system the father has already abdicated his parenting role—usually as his daughter enters adolescence. Parenting "duties" are handed over to his wife, so when the pregnancy occurs this father says little or nothing regarding the crisis. His silence sends the message—"whatever." The end result is an abortion the young woman never wanted, but had no support to do otherwise.

Dr. Theresa Burke, coauthor of *Forbidden Grief* and founder of Rachel's Vineyard, a post-abortion ministry, has also examined the question of why Christian parents who once were clearly pro-life push or strongly encourage their daughter to have an abortion. "Some mothers of these young girls have had an abortion at an earlier time in their life," Dr. Burke commented. "There seems to be a need to involve or pull everyone else into your same life experience so as to normalize it. It reaffirms their earlier decision. The bigger the group, in this case—the group of abortive women—the lesser the guilt."[13]

Echoing this sentiment, Deena Crandall, director of the Pregnancy Resource Center in Evansville, Indiana, said, "These post-abortive mothers don't want to deal with their own pain, and if their daughter carried her child to term, they would have to face it head on. It is like they say to their daughters, 'I was too young; so are you. I did it; so can you. You're a big girl; you'll get over it.'"[14]

Another reason a parent will pick up the phone and make an appointment for their daughter at an abortion clinic has to do with avoidance of loss. Parents have dreams for their daughter and when the pregnancy happens, all seems lost. "Instead of working through the grief and loss of that dream so something else can come and take the place of it," Dr. Burke said, "they take control quickly to get their daughter back on course. Abortion, they feel, will put their daughter back on the road of the dream they had. They are invested in seeing the fulfillment of the dream they had for her life."[15]

A serious communication breakdown is another factor when grandparents participate in their grandchild's abortion, Dr. Burke said. "They may be reading their daughter wrongly. Her fear of disclosure and anxiety over dealing with the initial reality of the pregnancy is misinterpreted as not wanting the child. A father wants to protect his daughter from the reality of what she is facing, so he responds with, 'You don't have to do this. We will help you take care of this.'"

Kathy's mom, Joanna, when faced with her daughter's pregnancy and watching her struggle, said she went to a place she never thought she would. "We were embarrassed, hurt, and unsure how to help Kathy or what to do. Over the next few weeks, I did consider abortion in order to stop her hurting and to save us embarrassment. I had walked in pro-life marches and volunteered at our local center. But when all of these realities came raining down on us, it seemed like the only way out. I knew it was wrong. I knew abortion would only bring about more problems of its own. But in those early frightening and uncertain moments, it seemed like the only answer. Had we done that, we would have lost not one, but two grandchildren, because Kathy was carrying twins."

A young, frightened, pregnant daughter is extremely vulnerable to accepting fault and blame. She is quick to appease the ones who are also touched by the situation, Dr. Burke points out. What parents might interpret as agreeing to the abortion is sometimes only a girl's attempt to regain parental favor. "She agrees to an abortion thinking, 'I will sacrifice myself and my baby in order to stop the conflict,'" Dr. Burke says. "All the while, she is screaming inside, 'Don't kill my baby!'"[16]

"The first words a pregnant girl hears from her parents has a tremendous impact on the future," Deena Crandall asserts. "It is huge."[17] During a retreat held at Rachel's Vineyard, post-abortive women were asked to describe what their ideal moment of disclosure to their parents would have been like. One woman wrote of her fantasy: "I imagine that with the telling, they would have come over to me, held me, and cried with me. I imagine that they would have assured me that everything would be okay—and that they would have said to me, 'You'll make a great mom.'"[18]

For this young lady, and thousands like her, the fantasy reaction didn't happen. She was left feeling that abortion was her only choice.

Numerous research studies have examined the reasons why young women chose abortion. Studies indicate that over 52 percent of them surrender to the procedure due to parental or boyfriend pressure.[19]

the model of the lie

Behind the act of abortion is something much deeper. It has to do with believing a lie, planted by the Enemy of our souls, and acting upon that lie. One Scripture clearly points out the agenda of the "father of lies."

> So the great dragon was cast out, that serpent of old, called the Devil and Satan, who *deceives* the whole world; he was cast to the earth, and his angels were cast out with him. Then I heard a loud voice saying in heaven, "Now salvation, and strength, and the kingdom of our God, and the power of His Christ have come, for the *accuser* of our brethren, who accused them before our God day and night, has been cast down. (Revelation 12:9-10, emphasis added)

How does this look in the life of a pregnant girl, her boyfriend, and potentially their parents? The Enemy's job is to deceive first. Then he spends the rest of the girl's life and that of her family accusing them for what they have done.

Your Daughter's Lie	Your Son's Lie	Your Lie (as grandparents considering abortion)
My life will be ruined. No one will know. This will have no effect on me. This isn't a baby—it is tissue.	No one will know. This will have no effect on me. This isn't a baby—it is tissue.	What will people think of you now as a parent? You can get rid of this embarrassment—no one will know. You have failed. Think of the shame when people find out.

A young woman, her boyfriend, and their parents believe the lie and act upon it. After the abortion, Satan returns as the accuser, tormenting the guilty with voices of condemnation.

Your Daughter's Voices	Your Son's Voices	Your Voices
You are a Christian and killed your baby. There is no way God can forgive you. You are a murderer.	You are a Christian and took your girlfriend to kill your baby. You failed to protect your baby. You are a bad person.	How could you have allowed your grandchild to be aborted? God will never forgive or forget. You are a horrible person.

And this is Satan's short list. What follows in a young woman's or young man's life and that of the participating family members is inevitable. As the tormenting voices come (and they always do), tremendous conflict grows within. This conflict creates a separation from self, family, and God. The ultimate result is *dis-ease,* which manifests itself in many different forms, from physical to emotional and relational problems.

how abortion may affect your daughter

In her article "Abortion in the Church: The Untold Story," Nancy Hird asserts that many Christians have bought into believing that even though a baby dies in an abortion, the procedure will save the woman. Research, on the other hand, shows that abortion almost always causes psychological and emotional damage. Not every woman experiences every symptom, and the onset of symptoms varies, as does the recognition that abortion is the root cause. "Christians, because they know it's wrong, are at high risk for psychological distress," Hird writes.[20]

Sydna Masse, a Christian attending a Christian college when she aborted, says that abortion starts a firestorm in a woman's soul. "After the abortion, Satan's intense attack begins," Masse says. "'God wouldn't want us,' abortive women say to themselves. After my abortion, a wall went up between God and me. I isolated myself from Christian society. I began drowning my feelings with drugs and promiscuity."[21] Masse's response is common.

According to Trudy Johnson, a post-abortion counselor with a national ministry, abortion can also have severe physical consequences. A link to breast cancer has been documented in numerous studies.[22, 23, 24] Renowned New Jersey breast cancer surgeon, Angela Lanfranchi, M.D., F.A.C.S., told the Coalition on Abortion/Breast Cancer in September, 2002, there is sufficient evidence to establish a cause and effect relationship between abortion and breast cancer. She explained that scientists use six criteria to decide whether there is a causal relationship (and not just an association) between a particular factor and a disease and that, in the case of the abortion-breast cancer research, all six criteria have been met.[25]

Other complications threaten the physical health of the post-abortive woman, according to other researchers. National statistics on abortion reveal that 10 percent of women undergoing induced abortion suffer from immediate complications, of which one-fifth (2 percent) were considered major.[26, 27, 28, 29] Over one hundred potential complications have been associated with induced abortion. "Minor" complications include: minor infections, bleeding, fevers, chronic abdominal pain, gastro-intestinal disturbances, vomiting, and

Rh sensitization. The nine most common "major" complications are infection, excessive bleeding, embolism, ripping or perforation of the uterus, anesthesia complications, convulsions, hemorrhage, cervical injury, and endotoxic shock.[30]

Still, some women do walk away from abortion clinics with no physical consequences. Some walk out and say there are just no emotional consequences, no regrets. Why do some women walk out of abortion clinics and feel no regret? Researchers investigating post-abortion reactions report only one positive emotion: relief.[31] Many are relieved of what they perceived to be an enormous threat in their life. The procedure is over. The problem is gone.

Temporary feelings of relief, however, are frequently followed by a period of emotional "paralysis," or post-abortion "numbness." Like shell-shocked soldiers, these post-abortive women are unable to express or even feel their own emotions. The focus is primarily on having survived the ordeal, and they are at least temporarily out of touch with their feelings.[32]

Studies within the first few weeks after abortion have found that between 40 and 60 percent of women questioned report negative reactions. Within eight weeks after their abortions, 55 percent expressed guilt, 44 percent complained of nervous disorders, 36 percent had experienced sleep disturbances, 31 percent had regrets about their decisions, and 11 percent had been prescribed psychotropic medicine by their family doctor.[33]

Even long-time advocate of abortion, Dr. Julius Fogel, a psychiatrist and obstetrician, insists: "Every woman—whatever her age, background or sexuality—has a trauma at destroying a pregnancy. A level of humanness is touched. This is a part of her own life. When she destroys a pregnancy, she is destroying herself. There is no way it can be innocuous. . . . Often the trauma may sink into the unconscious and never surface in the woman's lifetime. But it is not a harmless and casual event as many in the pro-abortion crowd insist. A psychological price is paid. It may be alienation; it may be pushing away from human warmth, perhaps hardening of the maternal instinct. Something happens at the deeper levels of a woman's consciousness when she destroys a pregnancy. I know that as a psychiatrist."[34]

Many of these women move into denial of the reality of what abortion meant and remained parked there between seven and ten years following their abortion, says Trudy Johnson. It is simply too painful to directly face what they have done. If they deny it, it feels like God doesn't know either.[35]

During this lengthy period of denial, the woman may go to extraordinary lengths to avoid people, situations, or events that she associates with her abortion. She may even become vocally defensive of abortion in order to convince others, and herself, that she made the right choice. But the "safe place" of denial begins to crumble at some point. When the walls of self-protection come crashing down, what happens next has been documented in hundreds of studies and also in anecdotal literature. These consequences include: depression, anxiety attacks, eating and sleep disorders, self-destructive behaviors, dramatic personality changes and suicidal tendencies, to cite just a few.[36, 37]

Teenage females are especially likely to experience post-abortion distress. One study found that one out of every three teenagers who aborted showed signs of emotional aftermath. Another study reported that less than one-fourth of teens who aborted were able to cope with the aftermath of their abortion in an nondestructive manner.[38] "Because of their limited experience, their greater dependence on others, and their youthful idealism, teenage women are extremely vulnerable to coercion, deceit, and compromised decision-making,"[39] writes David Reardon.

how abortion may affect your son

Richard was an honor student and a talented basketball star when his world turned upside down. A phone call the summer before he started college changed his life. It was his girlfriend. She was pregnant.

Richard did what many of his peers had done—he talked her into getting an abortion. "Parenting was the furthest thing from our minds, especially mine," he explains. "I really believed that abortion was the responsible thing to do. I took her down to the clinic, and she had the abortion."

It wasn't until the following Christmas that the impact of what he had done crashed down on him. "I walked into a toy store with my nephew and heard a baby crying," Richard recalls. "I crumbled inside. My heart felt like it had broken. I literally began shaking. I didn't know what was happening to me." Ultimately, guilt and shame led Richard to seek counseling from a pregnancy resource center where his girlfriend has also gone for help. He learned about God's forgiveness and became a Christian.

Another man was twenty-one years old and a junior in college when he began a relationship with a woman on campus. "The relationship fell apart, but a few weeks after it ended, she informed me she was pregnant," Don said. "When I learned she was considering abortion, I protested. I tried to persuade her not to go through with it, but I lost the battle. Now, if I am out in public and see a father holding a baby, a lot of painful stuff wells up in me. I go from incredible anger to heart-wrenching sadness."

Whether a young man was an active participant in the abortion or given no say over the life of his unborn child, emotional and relational consequences usually emerge. Society is not sympathetic to abortion survivors in general (post-abortion syndrome is still not recognized by the American Psychiatric Association), and men are virtually ignored when it comes to abortion. These "forgotten fathers" are not only stripped of their fundamental right to protect their unborn children, but their grief is not validated by a society that paradoxically demands accountability from the deadbeat dad but scorns the one who wants his child to live.[40]

For a man who has experienced the loss connected to abortion, the most consistent and evident symptom is anger, says author Bradley Mattes in his brochure "Men Hurt, Too." In his frustration over not being able to protect his baby, he may turn to alcohol or drugs to dull the pain. He may become a workaholic. The relationship with the mother of his aborted child almost always fails, and, as a result he may be unable to enter another. Other symptoms, Mattes says, include nightmares, panic attacks, and sexual dysfunction.[41]

"We have focused on the loss of life of the children and the emotional, physical, and spiritual loss to the mothers," says Jim Pye, "but we have failed to address to any great degree what young men lose to abortion. When a man's complicity, complacency, or the tragic lack of legal recourse results in the killing of his child, he has lost the treasure of his fatherhood."[42]

According to Wayne Brauning, founder of Men's Abortion Recovery

Ministries in Coatesville, Pennsylvania, abortion "rights" come neatly packaged with two lies: (1) abortion is a woman's issue only, and (2) the death of the unborn is not a real death. By accepting both lies, men who have lost children to abortion already have two strikes against them when they are confronted with their loss. Strike three is called when men neglect their own healing to console the woman, rather than express their own feelings of anger, hurt, or betrayal.[43]

what do grandparents need to consider?

"Abortion," writes Dr. Theresa Burke, "is a tragic attempt to escape a desperate situation by an act of violence and self-loss. Abortion is not a sign that a woman is free, but is a sign that she [and her family] are desperate."[44]

In the process of examining the issue of abortion, I asked several individuals who work with post-abortive women or men what questions they would like to ask parents who are considering abortion as a solution for their daughter's unplanned pregnancy or that of their son's girlfriend. One of the first questions Trudy Johnson said she would like to ask parents is, "Do you have an understanding of the long-term effects this may have on your daughter or son?" A second question is, "Are you prepared for how this abortion decision will affect your relationship with your daughter or son?" Johnson said she has observed so much brokenness and deep heartache in families where abortion is chosen. "There is an incredible amount of anger on the part of the daughter if she felt compelled to comply. Once the reality of what abortion really means hits that girl's parents, there are overwhelming feelings of guilt and shame. Both are dealing with grief and loss."

A third and equally critical question Johnson would like to ask is "What do you think your child will learn spiritually from the abortion experience?"

"What parents in the midst of this incredible crisis fail to realize is that how they work through this issue will leave an indelible imprint on the heart and mind of their daughter or son," Johnson commented. "Parents who have spent a lifetime teaching their child good and godly responses to situations will lose all credibility with that child if an abortion is chosen." From that point on, whenever a decision about a matter is required, a child is not as likely to ask himself or herself, "What does God say about this?" Rather, they will ask, "What is most expedient? What is the path of least resistance?"

Deena Crandall says a common misconception is that if an abortion is done early, there will be no effects for the daughter, son, or for the parental relationship. People believe this because they think that there is no attachment to the unborn child. A question Crandall would like to ask parents who are considering an abortion is this: "Are you prepared for the reality that this will never go away? When your first grandchild is actually born, there will always be the reminder that there was another."

Peggy Hartshorn, founder and executive director of Heartbeat International, would like to ask parents to consider very seriously what other options might be available. "I know you love your daughter," Hartshorn would say to them, "and you want to do what is best for her. But do you realize that abortion is never a choice made because of love? It is a choice made out of desperation, fear, or hopelessness."[45]

Hartshorn would also remind parents that they have time. "I would ask them to talk to people, to pray about it. I would like them to know that their decision might be entirely different if they just slow down."

IN SUMMARY

Abortion is a decision that cannot be changed. The choice is one that is made for many reasons, including:

- Threat of the loss of a future college education
- Threat of rejection by parents or boyfriend
- Threat of financial insecurity
- Threat of the loss of a lifestyle previously enjoyed
- Threat of the loss of respect and reputation if the pregnancy was known
- Threat of loss of identity and sense of self

Why do parents push their pregnant children to abort a grandchild? The reasons are tough to consider:

- Selfishness
- Shame
- Fear of rejection by peers
- Past personal experience of abortion
- Desire to avoid loss

Research and real-life experiences of men, women, and families clearly indicate that there are long-term and devastating effects of abortion—physically, emotionally, spiritually, and relationally. If you are reading this chapter and are considering an abortion for your daughter or are encouraging your son to push for it, answering the questions below might help you to see the long-term picture more clearly. Please look at the risks in light of your fear. Step back. Allow God's plan to unfold in your son's or daughter's life. In nine months, so much can change. Dear friend, you have the gift of time.

questions for REFLECTION and DISCUSSION[46]

1. What is it that you fear most about your daughter giving birth to your grandchild?
2. What is it that you fear most about your son in the role of father to your grandchild?
3. What is your greatest concern about your daughter's or son's ability to cope with the abortion decision now that you have learned the risks?
4. What reasons would you have for risking the long-term effects of abortion on your child, yourself, or your family?
5. What pressures do you think are leading you to consider abortion as the only option?
6. What happens when you stand back and ask yourself, "How will I feel about this decision five years from now? When another grandchild is born?"

wrestling with what to do

5

COULD ADOPTION BE AN OPTION?

> One of my most peaceful issues about the adoption plan for my grandson is that I know who he is with. I know the heritage that he will be acquiring and the love that he will have. I know that his family will stay in touch with us at some level.
>
> ELLEN, A BIRTH GRANDMOTHER

"CASSANDRA, MY OLDEST daughter, was a single parent of a four-year-old when she found out that she was pregnant again," Ellen began. "She came to me and told me of the situation. She frantically let me know that she couldn't parent this child; she was overwhelmed with her life as it was. I had already done much of the parenting for Jeremy, and I was immediately deeply concerned about this child's future and what part I would need to play.

"My first thought was, *Of course it is my responsibility to step in to parent this child.* Yet I was a widow of only two years with a high school sophomore at home. I wrestled with what was the good, noble, and right thing to do.

"I felt that I had no one to talk to because the people I would have gone to, especially in my family, had never been faced with this type of decision. As time went on, the decision came through answered prayer. God walked with me on my journey of realization—from 'I should do this' to 'I can't'—and brought me to a place of incredible peace.

"Along the way I realized, first, that as a grandparent I was not equipped physically or emotionally to parent another baby. Getting started was one thing, but being able to follow this through to completion was another.

"Second, as an educator and day care/school administrator, I have seen many children being raised by grandparents because it was the 'socially noble' thing to do. I also observed that many of those children were kept at an emotional distance. I have seen children suffer because they were not able to develop to their fullest potential. They were not talked with or played with enough. This soon-to-be-born precious child did not need to be parented by a single grandmother. He needed a two-parent family.

"Cassandra's decision was clear. She could not parent this child. My decision was also clear. I couldn't either. At that point, we explored adoption.

"Finding adoptive parents for my unborn grandchild was, in my mind, a monumental obstacle. I had never had experience with this type of circumstance before. I didn't know where to turn.

"A few months into the pregnancy the answer came. Through my teenage daughter and mutual acquaintances, we learned of a family living in another city that was waiting for a child. In a matter of just a few days, God removed what felt like an insurmountable obstacle. He replaced the impossible with the promise of possibility. God brought a settled peace into our lives.

"Working through an adoption agency, Cassandra met and talked with the adoptive parents at length. Although the contacts were awkward at first and painful, she wanted to be totally honest with them about how she had handled her life up to that point. She wanted to give them as much information as possible.

"All of us were at the hospital when Shawn was born. I needed that for a sense of closure—a marking point from which to move on. I needed to see, touch, hear, hold, and, above all, pray the blessings of God on my soon departing grandchild. Sometimes we have a lifetime to find the best gift to give, but occasionally we give the gift of a good life while letting go. I risked my anticipated personal pain and have a memory now that no one can take away.

"Since that day, I have received pictures from Shawn's family following special occasions or holidays. Recently the family visited in our area, and for the first time in four years I saw my grandson in person. I watched Shawn and his father walking up the church stairs, hand-in-hand as they entered the sanctuary. My heart was truly at peace. I know that we made the very best decision for that cherished youngster. Of course I miss him, and of course I think about him very often. But I am okay, truly okay. I know that God has placed this little boy into a family where he can grow into the man he is intended to be."

the changing face of adoption

In the 1940s–1970s, when a young woman was confronted with an untimely pregnancy, the legal choices available to her were only two: adoption or marrying the birth father. Societal and political changes over the past thirty-plus years have resulted in a dramatic change in options. The top three choices now most widely made by unwed mothers are abortion, parenting alone, or marrying the birth father.

Why has the decision to adopt "lost out"? Along with the legal abortion option has come a dramatic cultural shift regarding single parents. It has become socially acceptable for a single mom to parent her child. Fatherlessness is not generally thought of as a big deal anymore. Another reason why the adoption option is not readily chosen is that most families facing an untimely pregnancy have not had experience with adoption, nor do they know families who have made that decision. Misconceptions about the adoption experience abound. According to Anne Pierson, executive director and founder of Loving and Caring, the adoption choice for birth parents and their family members has been radically reframed in recent years. "Years ago, we didn't allow the birth mother and father to have a part in choosing the adoptive family for their child. They had little if any part in making decisions. Today, they are very much involved in that process."[1]

Adoption practice has shifted from a paradigm of totally closed to varying degrees of openness and contact before and after placement. Closed adoption, most familiar in American society, was not originally common practice. Prior to the 1920s most adoptions were open. Families knew where their children were. For a number of societal reasons, adoption records were closed, sealing off the flow of information and possibility of contact between birth parents, adopted children, and their adoptive families. Today, however, the adoption experience can be, and usually is, quite different.

According to Kathy Baer, director of Domestic Infant Adoption at Bethany Christian Services, the primary changes are reflected below.[2]

THE PAST	THE PRESENT
Birth parents had few rights.	Birth parents can develop a plan with which they are comfortable. Birth parents have rights, such as: • selecting a couple from written/picture profiles • meeting adoptive parents before or after the birth • negotiating the amount of contact after placement (pictures, letters, videos, visits).
Adoptions were done without birth father consent.	In most states, birth fathers must be fully informed.
Adoption records were sealed—no information was shared or contact ever made.	Most states allow for a degree of openness. Information about birth parents and adoptive families are openly shared and exchanged.
Lack of contact with the child. The baby was often whisked away after birth, never to be seen by the birth family again.	Both birth parents and birth grandparents often actively participate in the birth/hospital experience.
Focus was on the adopting couple's need for a baby. The baby was located for them by an agency.	Greater focus is placed on the birth parents' and baby's needs. Families are located and chosen for the baby by the birth parents.
Birth mothers were told to forget.	Relinquishment is recognized as a life-long process.
No counseling was provided for birth parents.	Counseling is available from the beginning through post-relinquishment. Most agencies provide post-adoption support groups for birth parents and birth grandparents.

Openness in adoption refers to a continuum within relationships that can exist between members of the birth family and the adoptive family.

Openness may include knowledge of information about the "other" family of the child, the birth parents' selection of an adoptive family for the child, contact through a third party, and, in some situations, ongoing visitation between the child and his or her birth family.

Betsy and Kenneth are three-year-old twins. They entered their adoptive home at four days old. Prior to their birth, their birth mother and birth father selected an adoptive family and met them on several occasions. Kathy, the birth mother, now lives in a different city but feels very free to contact the children's parents two or three times a year to check on the children. So does Matt, the birth father. Once a year, Susan, the adoptive mother, sends pictures to both Kathy and Matt, which they in turn share with their parents. This arrangement has worked beautifully for this family.

Because research has shown that some level of openness and communication between birth families and adoptive families makes for a more positive adoption experience for everyone, including the child, most agencies today are committed to promoting openness. It is important to realize that openness in adoption does not mean "coparenting." It means that birth families play an active role in choosing the adoptive family and, after "passing the parenting baton," have the opportunity and joy of knowing how the child is progressing through updates, pictures, and varying degrees of visitation in the years ahead.

common misconceptions

At least one other reason that the adoption option is not considered as often as it could be has to do with misconceptions of birth parents—about what their decision says about them and about their parents who support it. Imagine a young woman sitting in a restaurant sharing with her friends that she has decided to make an adoption plan. What type of responses is she likely to hear?

- How can you separate from your own flesh and blood?
- I could never do that!
- How do you know the parents you choose will be good parents?

- How could you do this? A mother who really loves her baby would never consider putting him up for adoption.
- Adoption is irresponsible—a cop-out.
- You will never be able to live with yourself if you do that.
- No one will be able to love your child as you would.

Now picture that young woman's mother and father sitting in the same restaurant weeks later, sharing with their friends about their daughter's or son's plan. What type of responses might they hear?

- How can you separate from your own flesh and blood?
- I could never do that!
- How do you know the parents your son or daughter choose will be good parents?
- How could you do this? Families who really love their children would never consider putting them up for adoption.
- What type of grandparent could let a child go? Are you just thinking about yourself?
- You will live to regret this. You will never know what happened to *your* grandchild.

These responses reflect an uninformed perspective of what adoption really means and what it says about the birth parent and his or her parents—the birth grandparents.

what the adoption decision says about your son or daughter

James Gritter, prolific author and practitioner in the field of adoption for over twenty years, says that the adoption decision says a lot about the character and values of birth parents. "Pregnancy at an inopportune time in life raises complex moral questions. I believe we learn at least as much about the moral strength of these folks from the way they work through their situations as we do from the circumstances leading to their pregnancies."[3]

In his sensitive and insightful book, *LifeGivers: Framing the Birthparent Experience in Open Adoption,* Gritter says the following about the birth parents' decision and what it says about them.[4]

BIRTH PARENTS BELIEVE CHILDREN BENEFIT FROM EARLY LIFE STABILITY.

Although many people hold that babies are endlessly adaptable, mothers who choose adoption for their children have a different perspective. They are convinced that children benefit from consistency and believe adoption is the course that offers the greatest consistency. They want to do everything they can to maximize their children's chances for a good life and are unwilling to settle for marginal circumstances.

BIRTH PARENTS BELIEVE IN THE IMPORTANCE OF FATHERS.

In contemporary times, this belief sets them apart. In contrast to societal nonchalance about fathers, birth parents believe fathers play vital, indispensable roles in the lives of children. (See chapter 3 for more extensive discussion of this issue.)

BIRTH PARENTS ARE REALISTIC AND FORWARD LOOKING.

Everyone loves to fuss over babies, but not everyone has the patience and energy to deal with the toddlers and teenagers they become. In many instances, birth parents have an unusually keen sense of the realities that lie ahead, coupled with rare honesty about their ability to follow through and unresentfully meet the formidable challenges associated with parental responsibility.

BIRTH PARENTS HAVE THE STRENGTH OF CHARACTER TO FOLLOW THROUGH ON THEIR BELIEFS.

The reality of pregnancy powerfully tests opinions about pregnancy outcomes formed in comfortable abstraction. It is not unheard of for people to set aside prior beliefs in the face of the pressure of an untimely, awkward, or unsupported pregnancy. Birth parents courageously translate their beliefs into action. Conviction causes them to take the road less traveled.

what the adoption decision says about birth grandparents

Bonnie, the birth grandmother of Chloe, talked about people's reaction to her decision not to take a major role in helping her daughter parent a second child as she did her first. Her daughter decided to make an adoption plan for Chloe.

"I had people call me and ask me, 'How can you do that? We'll take her,'" Bonnie said. "It was like they thought I was disposing of this child . . . like I didn't love her." Nothing could be further from the truth. "My daughter," Bonnie continued, "was already a single parent of one child, and was drug-addicted when her second baby was born. Chloe was born drug-affected, with significant health issues. Before we decided firmly on adoption, Chloe came home from the hospital with us. My friends watched me wean her off of the drugs still in her system. They watched me lay my life down for her and couldn't understand the dichotomy. They would ask, 'How can you do all that and then let her go?' I knew I could nurture Chloe back to health, but I also knew that I couldn't carry that responsibility for a lifetime.

"Every time a 'commenter' responded to our decision, I saw it as an opportunity to open the eyes of these people to the truth about adoption. The most important consideration was what the very best was for this little one, not what my needs or my daughter's needs were. At first, they didn't know what to do with me; but my friends now understand that Chloe is with a two-parent, mature adoptive family that my daughter and I chose. The family sends us pictures and updates through the agency. My friends now feel free to ask, 'How is Chloe? How are things going? How are you doing?'"

Birth grandparents like Bonnie who walk through an adoption plan with their son or daughter demonstrate what the decision reflects about them.

BIRTH GRANDPARENTS ARE REALISTS.

They can see the big picture as it relates to their particular family situation. In light of that bigger picture, they are able to support the decisions of their children that will bring about the very best outcome for their grandchild over his or her lifetime.

Kathy Baer, who has counseled birth parents and birth grandparents for nearly twenty years, says, "Birth grandparents in the midst of an adoption experience have not bought into the cultural message of quick fixes and no pain. Sometimes in the Christian world we follow the equation that if it is the best decision, the right decision, or God's will, we will have instant peace. Realistically, however, following God's will and making the right choice in a situation may mean pain and heartache in the beginning. Often the 'peace' comes later down the road when you can gain a different perspective and have given yourself permission to grieve the loss."

Tony and Mary assumed almost from the beginning that they would be parenting their daughter's baby. Amy assumed so as well. "We had friends who had adopted their own grandchild because their daughter was not equipped," Tony commented. "Coming from an Italian background, my grandchild was very important to me. It was natural to begin thinking in terms of raising this child, even though it meant that at sixty, we would have a ten-year-old. At this early stage, we had no idea about adoption. In fact, at that time I would have considered adoption a foreign concept; I wouldn't have even entertained the idea."

Clear communication between Tony and Mary regarding plans for the unborn child was, however, nonexistent. They both made assumptions about what the other was thinking that over time proved false. "We didn't talk very much," Tony admitted. "My thought was that we would do whatever we had to do. I didn't understand that Mary had some reservations about raising this child."

While Tony was on the parenting path, Mary's concerns were mounting, but remained unspoken. "This situation triggered memories," Mary said. "My sister and her husband died together in a car accident when they were twenty-six, leaving a young son. I can vividly remember watching my fifty-five-year-old mother walking a five-year-old to kindergarten to start all over. 'That is going to be us,' I thought. I just couldn't believe that this was happening to us. I worried about having enough energy for the tasks ahead. I wondered how all this would fit with my friends and peers and the rest of my life. I was getting angry about our 'predicament,' but I hadn't shared my feelings with anybody because I wanted to do what I thought was the 'right' and 'moral' thing—step in and parent this child. After all, this was our *grandchild.*"

A visit from their son and daughter-in-law began to turn the tide for Tony and Mary, as well as for Amy. "Anthony and Susan started asking us hard questions," Tony said. "They kept holding our feet to the fire, really confronting us about this decision."

Mary recalled, "While the kids and our new grandbaby were with us, Gracie had a tremendous case of colic. She was not a happy baby. We spent the whole time passing her around. Anthony and Susan were up all night, and Amy was in the bedroom next to them. Gracie was crying nonstop."

For Amy, this was a critical point in her facing the reality of the situation. "Her brother took her quietly aside," Mary said, "and challenged her about what would happen in our lives if she passed the parenting responsibility to us. Amy later told us that Anthony said to her that she will be a good mom . . . a really great mom. But just not yet. He shared his concern about us and that she needed to make some unselfish choices for her baby and for her parents. He led her to a website about adoption." Amy followed through and decided to make an adoption plan for her unborn baby.

At first, Tony was very distressed. "But it finally dawned on me that I was interested in this child because it was my 'possession'", Tony said. "And that is not the right way to look at it. I had to think about what was in the best interest of this child, not the best interest of us. When I arrived at that answer, it was clear. This soon-to-be-born baby girl needed a young dad and mom who could meet her needs in every way for a lifetime. I had to ask myself, 'Can you live with that?'" Ultimately Tony became convinced that the adoption decision was in the best interest of his grandchild. "We not only could live with that decision," he said, "but we experienced God's incredible peace about it as well."

BIRTH GRANDPARENTS KNOW THAT THEIR ROLE IN THE DECISION-MAKING PROCESS IS CRITICAL.

Moving from grief and loss through anger to acceptance is a significant jour-ney that must be taken when making any type of decision for an unplanned grandchild. Wise and realistic parents resolve to proactively help their child through the decision-making process. Considering this important role, Debbie Hill, director of Christian Adoption in Coffeyville, Kansas, says that the birth grandparents' perspective and their personal influence "can make or break an adoption placement. . . . Their focus should be on what is the best, most beneficial, and most productive place for the child. What is the best possible option for their future, well-being, health, and happiness?"[5]

Naomi Ewald-Orme, director of Adoption Link, in Yellow Springs, Ohio, also points to the essential role the parents of a young adult play in the deci-sion making. "The bottom line seems to be the need for trust—trust from the birth grandparents that their child has made a decision based on love for the unborn child and concern for his or her future. I have never met a birth mother or birth father who hasn't thought through the adoption plan time and time and time again. The best support grandparents can provide is to trust that the decision is a solid one made with lots love and careful planning."[6]

BIRTH GRANDPARENTS DEMONSTRATE STRENGTH AND RESOLVE IN THE MIDST OF SUFFERING.

Birth grandparents who understand the emotional roller-coaster ride that occurs after the adoption decision is made can be essential to the family moving successfully through the relinquishment experiences. As they are able to offer firm, loving support for their daughter's or son's decision, even when the pain seems too much to bear, birth grandparents can help miti-gate the fragile, vacillating emotions their child is experiencing.

Of the love that is required in adoption James Gritter writes, "I am con-vinced this kind of love is not soft and cute. It's an awful form of love, a tough, tearful, costly version of love that rattles a person's core. It has a lot more to do with midnight pacing and tear-smirched journals than with frilly affectations. This is the sort of devastating love that redefines a person's life story, and it deserves far more than candy coating."[7]

Birth grandparents who support the adoption of their grandchild are willing to walk toward this kind of love and through it. They know their own child will be suffering. They know that they too will be experiencing loss. However, they know the adoption decision is the best for their grandchild. They will not attempt to fix their child's pain, but walk through it with them.

Mary was with Amy during the birth. "As an RN," Mary said, "I kept watching the monitor. Finally, after some very tense moments, our little girl arrived. I heard her cry. At that moment I started to let go because I knew that although this baby came through Amy, this baby was not for Amy."

Continuing, Mary shared what the final moments at the hospital were like. "It finally all came to a conclusion when we came to pick up Amy at the hospital. I was walking behind Tony as we came to Amy's room. I stopped to see the baby at the nursery. When I walked into the room, Tony was sitting at the head of the bed. Angie, the adoption worker, was going over the final papers with Amy. Amy, our precious Amy, was at a point she had never been. She started to cry and I saw her shrink into her dad's arms. 'Dad, I don't think I can do this,' she whispered to him. I saw him tighten his arm around her shoulder and say to her, 'We can do it together.' After the papers were signed, we walked down to the nursery to say good-bye."

BIRTH GRANDPARENTS DEMONSTRATE WISDOM IN LOCATING SUPPORT.

Birth grandparents who walk through this experience with strength and decisiveness demonstrate wisdom. They know that they cannot walk alone. "These birth grandparents have given themselves a great gift—that of good, objective counseling," Kathy Baer says.

For one family, taking that proactive step was critical to working through all the issues that presented themselves. "We differed in how we responded to Beca's adoption decision," Maria explained. "We would get alone and David would say, 'This is a really good idea, we need to support her in this.' However, I would have been happy to keep the child; my heart was already locked in.

"We went for counseling and discovered that we were diametrically opposed in our view of the child and what our relationship to that child was now. I already saw myself as this child's grandmother. David, however, had emotionally removed himself and said it felt like the whole experience was happening to someone else. The counselor listened to him talk and then looked at him and said, 'You are the grandfather, right now. You need to be part of this decision making now.'

"I think David compartmentalized it because it hurt so badly. Beca was doing the same thing. She wouldn't talk about the baby or let me touch her stomach. Had we not gone for counseling, the long-term outcome of the adoption might look very different than it does today," Maria concluded.

Kathy Baer asserts that no good adoption can happen unless all options have been fully and completely explored. "When a family explores the pros and cons of parenting, the pros and cons of adoption, and are able to look five, ten years out, then they are ready to ask this question: 'What is the very best I can give this child?' They will then have the assurance that the decision made is the best for the child, their daughter or son, and themselves."[8]

Many pregnancy resource centers are equipped to counsel with a young woman and her family regarding the options available to them. Locating an objective counselor through a resource center or adoption agency is a very practical step to take when making this lifelong decision.

preparing for adoption as the birth grandparents

Birth grandparents also need to prepare for all the unfamiliar events surrounding the adoption decision. Both Kathy Baer and Anne Pierson offer insight into this lifelong journey.

SELECTING AN AGENCY

As a family moves through this critical decision-making process, Baer says that finding the right adoption agency is essential. There are a number of things to ask and know:

• Do they have a commitment to place the child in a Christian home?

- What is the criteria or definition of "Christian" home? And how do they go about finding that out?
- Is this a reputable, licensed, professional agency? Can you ask for references?
- Does this agency provide plenty of options for the birth family— choosing the adoptive family, levels of openness, what the hospital experience will be like?
- Does this agency provide pre- and post-placement counseling for the birth parents and other birth family members? How long is this service available to the birth family?
- Does this agency have a significant network and reputation of working with other adoption agencies across the state and country?
- What does the adoptive family assessment process look like? Does this agency conduct a thorough home study? Does this agency offer training to adoptive families regarding the issues of adoption and openness?

SELECTING AND MEETING THE ADOPTIVE FAMILY

Most adoption agencies now give birth parents and their families the opportunity to select the adoptive family. Birth parents are asked such questions as "What characteristics do you want to see in your adoptive family? What would you like as the family composition—other children or only child? What type of lifestyle is important to you—stay-at-home mom, country or city living? What are your values and beliefs about child rearing, faith, and family?"

According to Baer, most agencies then offer the birth parents profiles of families that meet as closely as possible the criteria they suggested. After a family is selected, they have the opportunity to meet. "Contact before the birth helps build the relationship between the families," Baer stressed. Birth parents and their families and future adoptive parents meet in a variety of locations, from the adoption agency office to restaurants to parks.

PLANNING THE HOSPITAL EXPERIENCE

One of the advantages of working with a professional, licensed, and experienced adoption agency is that the birth parent counselor from that agency works directly with the hospital. Many pregnancy centers working with the family also do an excellent job. Many times, the pregnancy center and agency work hand in hand—the center supporting the birth family and the agency doing the legal work. All arrangements for the hospital experience—every detail—are handled by the birth parent counselor.

Birth grandparents Paul and Laura said that this experience provided a sense that the highly emotional process wasn't out of control, that someone would help them through it. "Our son and his girlfriend asked us to be part of the hospital planning meeting with their birth parent counselor," Paul said. "We listened in and offered suggestions when asked about such details as who would be at the hospital, who would not, who would be in the delivery room, and so on. Because the birth mother's parents did not live in town, our son's girlfriend asked Laura to be her 'mom' in the delivery room. It felt good to see our children getting to make these important decisions."

For Rick and Susan, being part of the decision-making process was also key to their being prepared. "Our daughter asked me to be in the delivery room and asked the adoptive parents to come to the hospital a few hours after the baby's birth," Susan shared. "When the adoptive family arrived in my daughter's room, they didn't immediately go over to the baby. They went to my daughter first, hugged her, and then turned to us and did the same. In that moment, I knew that they understood the magnitude of what was taking place in our lives."

PREPARING FOR THE EMOTIONAL TOLL

According to Anne Pierson, who has worked with birth parents and birth grandparents for over thirty years, "Birth grandparents are not often prepared for the intense bonding feeling they will have when they first see the baby. It will be a feeling they have never felt before. They are not often prepared for the grief that will come, too. Birth grandparents may have a harder time than the birth parents because the birth parents are usually better counseled and prepared."

Kathy Baer adds, "As much as is possible, we talk with birth grandparents about anticipatory grief. Even when a family has come to the adoption decision with good counsel and they know in their head that this is the right decision for this little one, they need to know ahead of time that their hearts will take over at the hospital."

There are occasions when the plans for adoption collapse at the hospital. "When adoption plans go awry at the last minute," says Baer, "it is because someone hasn't worked with this family to understand the screams of the heart that say, 'Parent this baby!' If the family truly understands that there will be extraordinary moments of ambivalence, they can weather this time emboldened with the knowledge that the decisions made prior to this moment are the right ones."

PLANNING FOR THE IMMEDIATE ADOPTION AFTERMATH

Following the birth and placement of the baby into the adoptive family, birth families must give themselves permission to take care of themselves, says Anne Pierson. "As soon as the birth mother is able, planning a trip away for the entire family is a good idea." Doing just that provided some respite for David, Michelle, and their daughter, Crystal.

"As soon as Crystal was able," David said, "we planned a week away. Crystal's favorite spot is Branson, Missouri. We had always gone there for family vacations. It held such great memories. We spent the week there, sometimes keeping really busy, other times making sure we had time to talk. One thing we didn't want to do was to pretend that this was all behind us now. We had some great times of laughing that week, but we all did our share of crying, too. I think it was a first step in bringing healing to our family."

Kathy Baer agrees that having some plans in place is critical. Some of those plans can be short-term, like the family trip, or longer-term, such as finishing high school, planning for college, getting a job.

PREPARING FOR EMOTIONAL "TRIGGERS"

One very important factor that birth families need to understand is this: Their child or grandchild will be on their hearts and minds for a lifetime. Those thoughts and emotions will be greater at times, lesser at other times.

Certain "trigger" events will bring the child to the heart and mind of a birth grandparent, and emotions will come flooding to the surface.

Trigger times for birth grandparents, Anne Pierson suggests, will be the child's birthday or family holidays. These are expected. However, an unexpected trigger can throw emotions into turmoil. For example, a comment from a friend or relative such as "I still don't understand how you could let your grandchild go" may trigger sadness, grief, or even guilt and a sense of failure.

Pierson says that using word pictures in times like these can be helpful. "I tell families who are broadsided by these 'trigger' events that it is like standing in the ocean. You are enjoying yourself, but all of a sudden a big wave comes and knocks you down and when you get up you have sand in your suit. It was unexpected and irritating. You think, 'I just want to get out!' The truth is, if you just stand there long enough, the ocean waves will wash over you and wash the sand away."

When unexpected emotional hits come, Pierson advises birth family members to "stand firm, allow the feelings to come, work through them, recognize them for what they are, and know that they will pass." Adoption is not a journey for which birth grandparents planned. But as they continue walking through it, they learn much about themselves, about their children, and most important, about God, who in the darkest of times, truly makes a way.

IN SUMMARY

The adoption decision says much about the character and maturity of birth parents.

- Birth parents believe children benefit from early life stability.
- Birth parents believe in the importance of fathers.
- Birth parents are realistic and forward looking.
- Birth parents have the strength of character to follow through on their beliefs.

It also says much about the character and wisdom of birth grandparents.

- Birth grandparents are realistic about their family situation.
- Birth grandparents know that their role in the decision-making process is critical.
- Birth grandparents demonstrate strength and resolve in the midst of suffering.
- Birth grandparents demonstrate wisdom in locating support.
- Birth grandparents prepare in advance for the realities and emotions connected to the adoption experience.

questions for REFLECTION and DISCUSSION

1. Describe the adoption decision-making process you experienced in your family.
2. What were some of the reactions you encountered? Your daughter? Your son?
3. How can you or did you plan for the hospital experience? The days following?
4. What thoughts and feelings have you experienced following the adoption?
5. How would you describe how you are doing now? Your daughter? Your son?

when your child becomes a parent

6

EIGHT CHALLENGES OF THREE-GENERATIONAL LIVING

> I knew when Alise came home, everything would change for us. Trisha was nineteen and had no experience with babies. I knew I would need to be a support to her, but learning the balance between stepping in too much or not enough was difficult for me.
>
> CATHY, A GRANDMOTHER

YOUR DAUGHTER HAS made the decision to parent her child. Your son's girlfriend has made that decision, too. What does this mean to you?

Five days after our grandson was born, Kristy's last quarter of her senior year in college began, and she was there. Finishing on time was incredibly important to her and to us for many reasons. She had only three classes to complete for her degree in social work. We wanted her to succeed as a college student, and now as a parent, as much as she wanted to succeed. We knew that for a period of time this would require a change in our schedules as well as an expenditure of emotional, physical, and financial resources.

Prior to Micah's birth, I prepared to take six weeks' absence from work to care for him while Kristy went to school. Following that, Kristy placed Micah in the care of two women from our church while she finished college. My husband and I had also agreed to provide financially for Kristy and Micah until she graduated and started work.

As we navigated those early weeks and beyond, we asked some critical questions—questions thousands of parents who experience unplanned three-generational living ask. When a new mother and her newborn continue to live with her parents or live in close proximity, questions arise for grandparents such as: What is our role now? How do we set boundaries and rules to maintain a healthy household? What impact will this have on our marriage, our finances, and our emotional and physical health? How can we "let go" and let our child grow into the responsibilities of being a parent? These are just a few of the challenges parents in this situation face.

challenge one: examining roles

Throughout your child's life, you have functioned in different roles. Some of those roles have been healthy, promoting emotional and spiritual growth. And perhaps, some of those roles have been risky or unhealthy and maybe have even prevented growth and maturity. "You can let this crisis serve as a wake-up call in your relationship with your child," says Dr. H. Norman Wright, author of *Loving the Prodigal*. "You can eradicate any unhealthy patterns that you have allowed to develop."[1]

ARE YOU A PLEASER?

What does a pleaser parent look like? At a parent support group, Jack and Karla identified themselves as pleaser parents to their daughter, Michelle. Although their twenty-two-year-old daughter and grandson lived in an apartment by themselves, Josh was more commonly at his grandparents' home than with his mom.

"The words 'No, we can't' were not part of our vocabulary," remarked Karla. "We wanted to keep our daughter happy, hoping we'd influence her lifestyle and decisions. So when she needed us to babysit, needed money, or whatever, we provided it. Few questions asked. Few strings attached. Of course, we learned over time that this didn't accomplish anything. It only exacerbated her inability to make good decisions. Only when a friend confronted us did we really understand that our 'pleasing' was enabling."

ARE YOU A RESCUER?

Sitting around a table at a parent support group meeting, Don and Judy came face to face with the reality that they were rescuer parents. They'd been rescuing their daughter all her life and it wasn't working. Sondra was now the single parent of a six-month-old, and she was living with them. Rescuing was becoming overwhelming.

"The evening we were confronted with our rescuing mentality it hit us hard," Judy said. "But it also eventually felt freeing." Don and Judy were listening to a speaker who described how he had habitually stepped in and "rescued" his son, Dan, from his problems. It started in elementary school. If his son forgot something, his dad would leave work, retrieve it, and take it to school. If his son failed to follow a timely schedule for school projects, Dad would stay up late helping him finish. This parent rarely used natural consequences as a teaching tool. Now his son was a teen father and didn't have a clue how to make life work.

"We realized that night," Judy continued, "that our parenting mirrored the speaker's. We knew we had to change."

ARE YOU A MANIPULATOR?

It's easy to fall into the role of manipulator, especially for parents who feel powerless and out of control. Through manipulation, parents attempt to assume the authority that belongs to God alone.

In her book, *Restoring Relationships with Your Adult Children*, Karen O'Connor writes, "Parents who don't get their way with a few well-chosen words usually escalate their tactics. They use repetition, silence, anger, verbal abuse, and brooding to wear down their opponent. Some even stoop to bribes."[2] Manipulator parents may resort to giving or withholding monetary or other rewards, O'Connor says. Manipulative parents are always trying to gain the upper hand and, as a result, their adult child feels too vulnerable in their presence. The result is usually withdrawal on behalf of the child, which often leads to an escalation of the parent's attempts to control.

How can a parent stop manipulating his or her adult child? First, by examining the motivation behind the behavior. Ask, "Why am I doing this?"

"Do I have needs here that must be fulfilled?" Another key is to pay close attention to words and actions. One grandmother said, "It was a hard thing for me to admit, but I needed to be needed, so I would manipulate my daughter into allowing me to care for my grandchild much more than I should have offered. I would say things like, 'You are so tired, you really don't have time to do all you need to do.' I corrected her much of the time and suggested, 'Why don't you just let me take care of her.' Ultimately, my daughter angrily confronted me and told me how my behavior felt to her. My words communicated to her that I didn't think she was an adequate parent. That was a wake-up call to me."

challenge two: establishing boundaries

Once a parent truly understands the importance of not enabling, rescuing, or manipulating, the next task is to establish healthy boundaries. Many parents have a sense of what should be done, but putting it in place is challenging.

One of the things David and I understood from years of working with families and children is the importance of attachment. From the beginning, we knew Micah needed his mother to respond to his needs. It was a balance, learning to be sensitive to Kristy's emotional and physical needs as she recovered from childbirth and returned to school, while not robbing her of the opportunity to be Micah's mom and establish that crucial attachment with her son.

Don and Cynda faced the same balancing act. They knew that when their daughter came home to live just before the birth of her son, there would be major changes. Katlin, a college graduate, had moved out of state and was dating the man she thought she was going to marry. An unexpected pregnancy derailed the marriage plans and he wanted her to make an adoption plan.

"Early on," Don said, "we had to think through the new situation. It was no longer Katlin, our child, coming home for a visit like she did when she was in college. As parents we knew that we couldn't have that 'visiting mentality,' waiting on her hand and foot. The college days of 'bring your dirty laundry and empty checkbook—we'll clean one and fill the other' were over. We had to figure out how this new arrangement was going to work for us. Our thinking centered on making sure our daughter would be responsible for herself and her son. We didn't want her to assume we were the automatic babysitters, but we also knew that she'd need breaks."

For Don and Cynda, communication continues to be the key to work through the difficult moments. "We had to learn how to communicate as adults," Don explained. "I told Katlin, 'If you are frustrated, don't become crabby for a couple days and leave us in the dark wondering what's wrong. You have to communicate.'"

Julie Parton, manager of Focus on the Family's Crisis Pregnancy Ministry, finds that many balancing concerns are related to the day-to-day care of the child. "Who is the boss? Who makes the decisions about eating, sleeping, what type of clothing to wear?" Parton often asks families. "It's very difficult defining who the boss is. Grandma thinks the child needs a sweater to go outside. Mom doesn't. Grandma thinks the doctor should be called. Mom doesn't. Mom lets the baby cry, and Grandma or Grandpa question that wisdom. Who's the final authority? It's one of the biggest challenges I hear."[3]

Tricia Goyer, one of the directors of Hope Pregnancy Center in Kalispell, Montana, and author of *What Every Teen Mom Needs*, has observed this same scenario. "It is like the baby is being parented by committee. Everyone feels that they need to have a say. Teen moms have told me, 'When I'm at the doctor's office the doctor talks to my mom about the baby, not me. It's like he doesn't see me as having anything to do with this.'"[4]

Jeanne Warren Lindsey, prolific author and founder of a teen parenting program in California, believes that most young parents really *want* to parent. "They need a lot of support and instruction, and it takes a lot of working through, but they want to do it themselves."[5]

Erv and Barbara, whose twenty-five-year-old daughter, Jennifer, experienced an unplanned pregnancy while living in another state and moved back home, found Lindsey's statement to be true. "Jennifer values her role as a mother highly and she has risen to the occasion," says Barbara. "She has become a great mom."

challenge three: setting rules

"We had been empty nesters for almost five years when Katlin moved back home," Don said. "Although she was in her midtwenties, her lifestyle and her way of doing things was so different from ours. Sadly, it was the small things that resulted in the most conflict."

Don and Cynda have learned that sitting down together and redefining responsibilities is key. "Some of our talks came after real blowups," Don said. "We had to go back and instruct Katlin about basic housekeeping, even though she was competent and capable. One time we left her dishes in the sink just to see how long it would take her to get the message. After a week, they were *still* there and I blew up. You don't want to treat your daughter like a child, but sometimes it seemed she slipped back there, perhaps out of her own need to be nurtured."

Barbara and Erv knew they needed to establish rules and responsibilities *before* their daughter returned home to live with her infant son. "The rules were simple," Barbara said. "Jennifer had to get a job and had to pay for Grayson's food, clothes, day care. We didn't make these rules for our own financial reasons, but because our daughter needed to know what the real world was like."

Barbara and Erv also stressed with Jennifer that if she wanted them to babysit it had to be planned ahead. They didn't want to fall into the coparent role. Jennifer had a good attitude and was helpful, but it was a mental challenge for Erv and Barbara to raise their daughter to the level of being the third adult in the house. "This meant she needed to participate more in the function of the household," Barbara said. "We all sat down and developed a plan, and Jennifer took over all the laundry and began planning the evening meals."

challenge four: protecting your marriage

Jeanne Warren Lindsey believes it is critical for grandparents to take care of themselves and their relationship. Even if your daughter does not live in the same household, the strain and stress can be almost as great.

"My husband and I felt cheated out of our time together," said Jill, mother of Traci, who was a college student when she became pregnant and chose to parent her daughter, Becca. "My kids were elementary school age when Dale and I got married, so we never had time together. We'd just gotten used to the empty nest when our granddaughter came along."

"Traci didn't live with us," Dale added, "but it seemed like her daughter did. Traci constantly asked us to babysit Becca. She wasn't taking responsibility. There are times when I would say to Jill, 'You must say no.' But the next time Traci asked, Jill would agree."

Because Dale and Jill approached the needs of their children and grandchildren differently, they experienced a lot of conflict. "I take the hard line when Jill doesn't," Dale said. "However, when Traci seemed to resent having Becca, what choice do you have? Do you send this little girl home if there is even the slightest chance of emotional abuse?"

Don and Cynda say they had a solid, mature marriage before Katlin arrived, but the new circumstances have cramped their ability to have time alone. "What we do now," Cynda says, "is go out of town every three months. We also participate in a weekly couple's Bible study. We attempt to maintain separate friends and do not feel we need to include Katlin in all our plans. We maintain some semblance of our private life. Yes, our relationship has been impacted, but we know we must balance our marriage needs to provide a healthy emotional balance for all of us."

challenge five: addressing the strain

Wanda, whose daughter's unplanned pregnancy propelled their family into change, says the emotional challenges can feel overwhelming at times. "I kicked a hole in the wall once," Wanda admitted. "My husband and I take turns being resentful. It's good that it usually doesn't happen at the same time! I feel quite judgmental of my daughter sometimes. I'm especially angry because her partner, and the father of two of her children, does nothing to contribute to the needs of the household. They live in an attached apartment. We are separated only by a door, which I leave unlocked. I do it for my grandchildren's sakes."

Bruce and Cheryl, whose daughter, Allison, was in college and moved back home to parent her daughter with support from her parents felt the physical and emotional strain as well. "My dilemma," Cheryl commented, "was that Allison didn't have a lot of time to herself since she worked nearly full time and was finishing school. I knew she needed a break and space to regroup. She needed to talk to friends and have a social life. I understood that need, but if my husband worked late and she did too, I didn't get a break. I was IT for Madison. Sometimes I just dreamed of being on the beach!"

Fortunately, Cheryl learned over time that she could not continue this way and remain physically and emotionally healthy. "I decided for the sake of all of us that I didn't have to be the 'martyr' here and that there were other options. One of those options was to plan one day a week when I would not have child-care responsibilities. Because Allison and Bruce both had to work, it meant that we needed to find a babysitter for one day a week. A simple inquiry at our church quickly resolved my need for time and space, and Madison is doing just fine."

challenge six: handling financial pressures

One of the issues discussed by all these parents involves financial pressure. The added responsibility of providing for the needs of their daughter and a baby, when it was not "in the budget," presents significant challenges.

"We took a financial hit when Jill made the decision to quit work and care for Becca," Dale said. "Traci initially placed Becca in day care, and we would pick her up if Traci was working late. But it got harder and harder emotionally to see where that little one spent her day. One time we picked her up at the caregiver's house, and amidst the chaos a guy came to the door with a cigarette hanging out of his mouth and our granddaughter in his arms. That was it. Making the decision that Jill should provide day care for Becca was a major lifestyle change for us, especially financially."

Dale said that what helped them the most was their attitude. "We knew that helping Traci with Becca's care was essential for Becca's welfare. We also knew it wasn't going to be forever. We sat down and took a hard look at our budget and made changes about how we spent money. Simple things like not eating out as much as we did and not accumulating things on the credit card helped more than one might imagine. Becca is now in school and Jill is back at work. The financial pressure was just a season of time for us."

challenge seven: letting them grow

Dr. Julie Parton urges parents to keep in mind that "the ultimate goal is to move your parenting child toward independence and to facilitate her in becoming the best mom she can possibly be. Maybe you can do it better, but remember the old adage, 'Give them a fish, they eat for a day. Teach them to fish, and they eat for a lifetime.' Equip her, but don't do it for her."[6]

"My daughter missed a lot of basic parenting cues," commented one grandmother. "She didn't pick up her son when he needed it. She didn't change him enough. Watching this happen was painful. She finally agreed to attend parenting classes at our local pregnancy resource center. She would listen to her mentor before she would listen to me. That was fine, because my greatest concern was the baby."

What are some other specific, practical things parents can do to address the challenge of facilitating their child's maturation and parenting skills? First, *plan ahead*. If the decision has been made by your daughter to parent her child, the reality of that decision is that you, as the grandparents, will be involved. In the months prior to the birth, planning ahead by asking and answering the following questions can help prevent surprises.

1. What type of living arrangement is possible? Is the house large enough to accommodate this growing family? What changes need to be made?
2. How can the young mother contribute to the household's monthly expenses? Is it realistic to think she can work part time? If she does, what about child care and related costs?
3. To what extent can family members participate in the daily care of the child?
4. How will the family handle discipline issues? Will the young mom resent their input?
5. What about the young mom's social life—dating, curfew, and personal freedom? How will these issues be handled?
6. Will the living arrangements have structure and allow space (emotionally and physically) for all involved?[7]

Second, make a contract, and redefine it over time (see page 117). After discussion, it's time to get the plan down in writing. This will help everyone remain focused. It will also keep communication clear and serve as a reference point when conflict arises.

By planning ahead and keeping communication open, the young parent will grow. Barbara says. "I have been able to experience wonderful joy watching Jennifer be an excellent mother to Grayson. She does not always make the same decisions I would make, but her level of love and caring are terrific. I have been able to see her use the best of what I have taught her. The experience has also brought us very close. She now respects me and my opinions in a way she never has before. She sees me able to accomplish some things with her son that she finds difficult, and she wants to know how I do it. I think she now understands how deeply she has been loved her whole life. She says she understands that your heart exists outside of you and gets up and walks with your child."

THE CONTRACT[8]

HOUSEHOLD NEEDS AND CHILD-CARE RESPONSIBLITIES	I will be responsible for the following:
Housecleaning. Include care of communal living area, bathroom(s), and individuals' rooms. Plan for handling baby clutter.	
Meal Preparation and Cleanup. Regular schedule plus anticipated changes after baby's birth.	
Laundry. Specify who does it, when, and how.	
Child care. Who takes care of the baby?	
Discipline. Who's in charge? Working out disagreements, how will that be done?	
Education. While parent is in school how will child care and transportation be handled?	
Medical Coverage. Health insurance or other arrangement for paying medical bills.	
Financial. Work plan for young parent(s). Responsibility for baby's expenses. Extent of assistance to be provided by grandparents.	
Teen Parent's Social Activities. Curfew. Contact with baby's father. Dating rules, use of car, telephone (limits to use and who pays).	
Music/Television. Define limits (if any) on volume, type of music or program, and timing.	
Changing the Contract. Procedure for contract changes.	
Signature. All household members.	

challenge eight: letting them go

In the life of every parent there comes a time to "let go." There is no question that the process of letting go begins early—almost with a child's first steps. A parent allows the falls and stumbles to occur so that the child will eventually become confident and independent. David and I worked at many aspects of letting go as Kristy grew into a young adult. When she left for her first year of college, we really understood that we had to release her. We realized we could no longer control the circumstances, events, or people that came in and out of her life.

However, when the pregnancy occurred and Micah was born, the letting go took on a different dynamic. Our daughter needed support, but how much was too much? It became a balance of stepping aside to let her grow up, but also walking alongside to encourage her in her new role as a mom.

One of my first lessons was to realize that Kristy was the parent, not me. I had to realize that Micah was Kristy's responsibility, not ours. Both David and I had to step aside and let Kristy grow and develop into the mother she wanted to be. We reassessed our dreams for our daughter and encouraged Kristy to create new dreams, for Micah's sake.

After graduating from Wright State University in Ohio with a degree in social work, Kristy obtained a job as a social worker in a large nursing home. By that time, Micah was in the care of a woman, Barbara Cullen, who has become his "heart" grandma. Four months after Micah's birth, Kristy moved into an apartment not far from us. We thought that was too soon—but it was her decision. At this point, especially, I needed to step back and allow Kristy to make decisions for herself and her son. Of course there were times, probably many of them, when I offered too much advice, or perhaps ignored a need I should have responded to, but this was a learning process for us all. We all grew as we tackled new challenges. There were many times that my heart hurt for my daughter, because I knew it was tough for her to carry the parenting responsibility alone. It was tough to deal with the financial load as well. We did help Kristy with day-care expenses, but I knew she longed for the day when she could make it solo.

What does it really mean to "let go" when it comes to your child and grandchild?

- To let go means that you take your hands off and truly allow God to work His way out in the life of your child.
- To let go means that you control your words and monitor your attitudes and place them under the authority of God.
- To let go means that you know you are not responsible for your child's choices and can step off the guilt mobile.
- To let go means that you must allow your child to truly learn from mistakes and misjudgments.
- To let go means you are no longer the "fixer" of all things.
- To let go means that you no longer "drop" everything you are doing to please your adult child.
- To let go means that you don't stop caring *about*, but you do stop caring *for*.
- To let go means that you recognize not only cognitively but experientially that God is working out His plan in your child's life, and "the plan" will not always go in the direction that you think it should.[9]

Dale and Jill say that Traci's unexpected pregnancy affected them relationally, financially, and emotionally, but not just in a negative way. "There have been some benefits that help offset the strain and tension of the situation," Dale says. "Our communication with our daughter has improved, somewhat by force, but it has improved as we have had to talk to each other about our granddaughter. Many times the discussions caused our daughter to think a little harder about how she was reacting to Becca. I believe that Traci has been a better mother because of the example we have been able to set for her. And the incredible blessing of being able to be a part of our granddaughter's life is immeasurable. The little child we were so concerned about has become a vital part of our relationship with each other as well as with our daughter. Even when we thought we shouldn't have her with us as much as she was, Becca brought incredible joy to our lives. Most of all, we believe that God has given us a second chance to be parents, only to do it better this time. We certainly didn't expect to be raising children at this age, but we find ourselves having more patience and self-control than we had with our kids. I think God knew what He was doing when He made us grandparents; it just didn't happen in the time frame we expected it to."

Don and Cynda agree. "We didn't plan this," Cynda says, "but we are willing to do what needs to be done for the sake of our grandchild and daughter. Our ministry is at home."

Don added, "Some days I wish we could go back to what we had. But I recognize that this is what God has brought us—the tremendous gift of our grandson. It's our chance to live out our beliefs. We pray that God will give us the grace to do it day by day."

IN SUMMARY

When a young adult becomes a parent before the time seems right, grandparents face many challenges. What do these challenges require?

- Parents will need to examine what roles they will take in the life of their young adult and in the life of their grandchild.
- Parents will need to establish healthy boundaries for the sake of all family members.
- Parents will need to set rules, perhaps new ones, so that all family members know what to expect.
- Parents will need to protect the well-being of their marriage.
- Parents will need to address the new level of strain and pressure within the household.
- Parents will need to handle financial pressures that result from added responsibilities.
- Parents will need to be proactive and supportive in letting their adult child grow and mature as a parent.
- Parents will need to learn how to let go of their child in a whole new way.

questions for REFLECTION and DISCUSSION

1. What role do you tend to play in your child's life? Pleaser? Rescuer? Manipulator?

2. What are the challenges you anticipate, or have experienced, in setting boundaries and balance in your home?

3. What rules and household routines will you, or have you, established to help your child grow into her role as an adult and parent?

4. How have you taken care of yourself? How have you taken care of your marriage relationship? How have you managed the needs of the remaining children in the home?

5. How have you managed the financial challenges?

6. After reading this chapter, what plans do you need to make for further positive action?

you didn't plan on a second shift

7

WHEN GRANDPARENTS BECOME PARENTS — AGAIN

> Never in our wildest imagination did we think that we would be starting all over again as parents at our age. However, when it became apparent to us that Kelly couldn't parent our grandson, we stepped forward. He had been part of our lives for almost a year, and this was the only option we could consider.
>
> SHERRIANN, A GRANDPARENT RAISING HER GRANDSON

IT WAS AN unplanned pregnancy. Your son or daughter made the decision to parent his or her child. Now there is a crisis. Your son or daughter—the child's parent—cannot fulfill the responsibility. It may be due to alcohol or drug abuse. It may be due to child neglect or abuse. It may be due to immaturity, unemployment, even domestic violence. For whatever reason, you as grandparents step in. You feel that out of love, duty, and deep bonds with the grandchild, you must. You offer a temporary safety net for your grandchild who would otherwise tumble into the child welfare system. Now that temporary plan has become permanent. Life has changed for you—for a lifetime. You are now on second shift.

David and Paula had enjoyed their empty nest for about six years. "Our son, Lee, was going through a divorce. He was very upset and in the process of the rejection he was feeling, he moved in with another young woman. About three months into the relationship, Amber was pregnant. Lee told us that she wanted to get an abortion, but we pleaded with her not to do it. We promised her we would help her.

"After Josh was born, she called us and reminded us that we said we would help. When Josh was just a few days old, she brought him over. We kept him a few days. She came back and took him home. But, when he was two weeks old, she brought him back and we have had him ever since.

"Why did we do it?" David said. "We did it because our son was not in a place to be a dad, and Amber's lifestyle created an unsafe environment for our grandson. After ten years of having varying levels of custody and being in and out of court, we were finally able to adopt Josh last year."

Phil and Angie's daughter was not doing well. She experienced an unplanned pregnancy at nineteen and insisted that she would parent her baby. "We tried to offer her all types of support and counseling," Phil said, "but Alicia walked away from us. She moved in with the baby's father and eventually married him."

About six months later Alicia and Greg started bringing Sydney over for Angie to watch during the day. "I run a day care in our home," Angie said. "Because Sydney had such terrible allergies which were exacerbated in our daughter's home by heavy smoking and the mold problems of an old house, Alicia started asking to leave her daughter with us for days on end. For Sydney's safety's sake, I felt I couldn't say no."

When the young couple's marriage broke up, Angie and Phil just kept their granddaughter. For well over a year there were no permanent plans for this little girl. Her parents were split. Her father was jobless. She had no health insurance. "Finally," Phil said, "we approached our daughter and the baby's father and asked, 'Why don't you let us adopt her? That way, she will have security, permanency, and health insurance.' That is what happened."

Ted and Susan never dreamed that after four years of being out of the daily parenting role they would be there again. Their daughter had left home at age twenty. Four years later she was heavily into drugs and alcohol, and her parents had lost contact with her. "Finally Jenny called and told us where she was," Ted said, "and that she had a baby. We urged her to come home and she did. As soon as she stepped off the airplane with Kristen, that little girl captured our hearts.

"They stayed with us a few days and then returned to their home. We would visit our daughter and her boyfriend (not the baby's father) occasionally, but it was so very difficult. Their home was a major hazard for Kristen in every way possible. Two years ago, something happened that changed our lives. We got a call from our daughter's boyfriend. He was afraid that Jenny was going to take Kristen to Chicago that weekend to sell her. She had seen a show on TV where someone had gotten $5,000 for a baby. We told Jim to get the baby out of there. Hide her . . . do anything . . . until we got there. We brought her home at twenty-two months. She could barely walk; she didn't know how to eat. She is now four years old and doing absolutely fine. Her adoption was final last spring."

These three families represent hundreds of thousands of grandparents in this country who, through the brokenness of their children's lives, have taken on the parenting role for their grandchildren. Sue Powell, adoption specialist with Montgomery County Children Services in Ohio, says that for most of the "second shift" parents, it starts as a temporary safety and security plan for the grandchildren. "They see the dysfunctional nature of what is happening or they are just dumped on. When they start providing all the care, they bond with these kids. They love their grandchildren. The birth parents don't get their lives together and the grandparents have to step in. They feel they have no other choice at that point."[1]

Josh's mom-grandmom, Paula, said, "We knew that we had to push to get some permanent arrangement for this little boy. He couldn't stay in limbo. As far as we were concerned, there was no choice in the matter. Everyone said that we had a choice . . . yes, but not one we could live with."

Powell explains that parents wait and wait, hoping that their children will mature; but for many, it doesn't happen. "Parents come to the realization they have to do something to protect the well-being of their grandchild. It is at this point that more stable custody options are often explored."

custody options

Many challenges face grandparents. One of the most difficult involves the court system. Custody options are confusing because the word custody means different things to different people. Prior to making any decisions about custody, grandparents should seek professional advice from a family law attorney to review their options.

Custody defines a relationship of control and decision making for a minor child. There are several types of custody: physical custody, legal custody, guardianship, and adoption. The following are general descriptions of the custody arrangements, but every state has certain guidelines that they follow.

physical/informal residency

This is an informal agreement that happens between the birth parent and grandparents without any involvement with the court system. Grandparents have no legal authority in terms of making decisions about the child. With informal residence the birth parents must take care of all legal actions such as enrolling their child in school and making medical decisions. In some states, however, through the use of the power of attorney, grandparents can gain the legal rights to make decisions on behalf of the child. This can be accomplished if the parents agree to this arrangement or if the parents' whereabouts are unknown. Unfortunately, this situation offers the least protection for grandparents and their grandchildren.[2]

temporary custody

In many circumstances, the grandparents step into a crisis with their grandchild, which requires a level of court action. In many states, that first step is called temporary custody. This is usually a one-year agreement, after which more permanent arrangements must be made. Barbara Fuller, program manager of the Center for Healthy Communities in Dayton, Ohio, advises grandparents in this situation to check with the county in which they reside to determine which court has jurisdiction in their situation.

legal custody/guardianship

Following the first step of temporary custody, grandparents may go to court to secure a more permanent arrangement for their grandchild. They may be granted what is called legal custody or guardianship. In most states, legal custody is handled in juvenile court. Guardianship is handled in probate court. It is essential for grandparents to check with their county regarding which court has jurisdiction.

These formal agreements mean that the grandparents assume legal authority to make all decisions related to the health, education, and well-being of the child. "Grandparents who obtain guardianship or legal custody have some important rights regarding the child," Fuller says. "They have the right to make day-to-day decisions for the child, attend school conferences, and make medical decisions without consulting the child's parents. Grandparents who hold legal custody or guardianship have control over when and how their grandchild sees his or her parents, unless a court-ordered visitation schedule exists. However, they do not have the right to determine the child's religion nor move the child out of state without the court's permission."[3]

adoption

The families who shared their stories in the opening of this chapter all eventually chose to adopt their grandchildren. For them, this option provided the most secure custody arrangement. When grandparents have legal custody or guardianship, court actions suspend their adult child's parental rights for a period of time. When grandparents adopt their grandchild, however, all legal ties to the child's parents are permanently terminated. Adoption, in the eyes of the law, places the grandparents as parents in the fullest sense of the word, giving them full responsibility for all needs of the child.

Even though adoption offers a lot of benefits to the grandparents and child, it is not generally the first option grandparents choose. The three families mentioned above did not pursue this option initially. One reason is that grandparents do not want to "give up" on their own children. "They don't want to have to say that their own child is a lousy parent," explains Margaret Hollidge of AARP's Grandparent Information Center. "They love their child and want to be loved by him or her. They hope there is just one more thing out there that will help him or her to be able to parent properly."[4] When an adoption occurs, it means that the last hope of their adult child getting his or her life together enough to care for their grandchild is gone.

Another reason grandparents do not pursue adoption initially is that they believe, erroneously, it is not necessary because the child is already a family member. They feel that adoption might be confusing to the child if the birth parent is still in the picture. Keeping the roles of mother and dad separate from grandmother and grandfather will make it less confusing, they assume.

A third reason that grandparents do not pursue adoption is because of the legal and financial complications that emerge. David and Paula found the whole connection with the court to be emotionally and financially draining.

"Josh's birth mother could not parent him, nor did she want to; but she made it very difficult for us to provide permanency for him. It was very demeaning. During custody hearings, if she said something negative about us, we were the ones that had to prove it wasn't true. In the beginning the court knew all about her lifestyle but ordered visitation anyway. Because she couldn't drive, we had to pick her up for visits. This went on for years and years.

"The system did not serve Josh or us well. On the last trip to court, Josh, at age ten, was asked to speak. He told the judge that his mom had three chances and that in his mind, she was 'out.' Finally, after ten years of emotional and financial challenges, we were able to adopt our grandson."

special challenges

As grandparents live the daily reality of second-shift parenting, it is important to know that others have been there and have dealt with the challenges. What are those challenges?

THE EMOTIONAL TOLL

Beth Brindo, adoption expert at Bellefaire Jewish Children's Home in Cleveland, Ohio, comments that grandparents who adopt must grieve the loss of the vision of their birth children as parents. They will not experience the joy of watching their children raising children. The bitterness that might accompany this grief can spill over into their communications with their adopted grandchildren about their birth parents and the circumstances surrounding their birth, potentially poisoning the children's understanding of their roots and their own self-esteem.

The relationship with the birth parents can also present significant challenges to adoptive grandparents. Because the grandparents know (and perhaps dislike or disrespect) the birth parents, will they be able to perceive the child as a person in his own right? Will they be constantly looking for evidence that he is "just like" his birth father? Will he have the same weaknesses as the birth mother?

Furthermore, grandparent adoption can include many of the same feelings and dynamics as an ugly, bitter divorce. For example, grandparents who may have suffered themselves as a result of the behavior of the birth parents may have great difficulty presenting the birth parents in a positive light to the child.

John and Catherine's twenty-year-old daughter, Rebecca, brought them their greatest joy and their greatest heartache. The year after she finished high school, Rebecca met a young man at the restaurant where she was working. She became involved with him, and over time it was obvious that she was in an abusive relationship, yet she refused to leave it. By the time she was nineteen, she was the mother of a beautiful son. However, addiction to drugs and alcohol took precedence over her care of Michael.

John and Catherine made the heartbreaking decision of reporting their only daughter to the protective service agency in their town so that young Michael could be safe. Rebecca's live-in boyfriend quickly talked her into signing the child into the legal custody of her parents. Eventually, John and Catherine adopted Michael.

Grandparents can feel anger, guilt, and shame, Margaret Hollidge says.

"They feel they have 'failed' with their own child. When their own child is in such a destructive lifestyle that it impairs their ability to parent, it feels like a death to them, and they grieve over and over again."[5]

Catherine agrees. "I cannot think of anything other than the death of your child that can bring such devastating heartache," she shared. "The day we called protective services will be a day I will never forget. I felt as though we had no choice. I felt as though we had relinquished any hope for our daughter getting better."

Part of the emotional toll includes anger about what has happened to their grandchild. Grandparents often must deal with damaged children, Hollidge says. "If the child is an infant, he may have been born drug-addicted and be going through withdrawal. Older children have a profound sense of loss, of rejection. They have low self-esteem. They think their parents have abandoned them and wonder what will happen if they lose their grandparent, too."[6]

PERSONAL LOSSES

When a grandparent steps into the parenting role the second time around, they experience great gains. Carol, who parented her granddaughter from birth and recently adopted her, said, "My greatest gain is knowing that she is safe and secure . . . and happy. She is so sweet and has given us so much love. I could never release her."

Yet for Carol and others there have been losses as well. "I have learned to be honest about those losses," said Marty, who is parenting two of her grandchildren. "The losses are real. I need to recognize them, process them, and move through them if I am going to be the parent Micah and Kayla need."

"One of the losses Paula and I experienced," commented David, "was some of our friends—people we used to do things with. They are in the grandparent stage and we are still parenting."

Catherine says that while many friends support her, others do not feel comfortable around children anymore. "Theirs are grown, and they will say, 'We'd love to have you, but please don't bring Michael.' That's hard sometimes, because I don't feel like I fit in anywhere right now."

For Carol, the greatest loss has been her lifestyle. "I really did grieve for the lifestyle I was giving up. With all our children out of the home, my husband and I really enjoyed the freedom we had. I had gone back to school to get a nursing degree. When Callie came, it was much, much harder to finish my education than I anticipated. As she got older, I put off as long as I could getting her involved in activities like dancing and athletics because I knew what it meant: My schedule would be dictated by hers."

Commenting during a meeting of grandparents who are parenting, David said, "Those of you with younger grandchildren are in for a shock because you will be controlled by a schedule you have long forgotten: parent-teacher conferences, school activities, sports events. You can't go on vacation whenever you want. There are a lot of things that tie you down. As grandparents now parenting a ten-year-old we have given up a lot. But I don't regret it for one minute. Jason is an awesome kid!"

Richard and his wife, Samantha, had looked forward to a complete lifestyle change that retirement would bring. Last year, after three years of hoping their daughter would improve, they finally filed for adoption of their four-year-old grandson. "We knew that this decision would change everything for us," Richard said, "but our dreams and wants paled in significance to Zack's need. The losses for me are actually ongoing—mostly the freedom I anticipated. I am approaching fifty-five with twenty-seven years on the job. I am near that magic thirty years. I am getting into the time bracket that I could cut those strings and go work for K-mart or some place like that. It would take a lot of stress out of my life. That certainly isn't the case now."

Samantha released some dreams as well. "We planned to build a retirement home in Gatlinburg," she said. "That was our dream and now it won't happen. We see that dream as gone—or at least significantly postponed."

FINANCIAL PRESSURES

"A big blow for many grandparents is what it costs to keep little feet in shoes these days, to provide everything from food to day care," Margaret Hollidge says.[7] Some grandparents take extra jobs. Others quit work to once again stay home with the kids.

"Perhaps my greatest stress," says one grandmother, "has been financial.

We had been living on our pensions, Social Security, and savings—and that suited us just fine. Now that our grandchildren have arrived, everything goes to food, clothes, and medical expenses. We are barely making it month to month."

Many grandparents are not aware that there are various ways to get financial help. In Appendix III, a list of helpful website resources for grandparents offers suggestions on how to deal with this potentially crippling issue.

BOUNDARY ISSUES

Many grandparent adoptions are also open adoptions. The birth parents know where the child is, and they continue to relate to some degree to the child and family. As in all open adoptions, adoptive parents must set some boundaries about the type of contact, timing of contacts, who holds parenting responsibility and decision-making authority, and information to be shared (how and when).

In discussing boundaries, family therapist Dr. Lenora M. Poe says: "Because of the love that grandparents have for their adult sons and daughters, they often have a difficult time setting appropriate limits and boundaries for them. Thus, when a son or daughter shows up (perhaps on probation from prison) a grandparent's authority with the grandchild may be quickly undermined by the son's or daughter's disruptive behavior.

"Some grandparents," Dr. Poe commented, "attempt to deal with this intrusion by involving the birth parents in some of the child's daily routines. When this fails, they can no longer deny their anger and frustration. When this happens the grandparent may be forced to say what they hoped they would never have to: 'You can't come here anymore. I have your children to raise. I can't raise you again and raise your children. You will have to stay away until you get your life together.'"[8]

principles of thriving — not just surviving

There is no question as to whether there are challenges for grandparents in rearing their grandchild. However, there are also positive principles to keep in mind that will help grandparents move through the experience with strength, understanding, and perseverance.

KNOW THAT *YOU* ARE THE PARENT

"Adoption within families is not without its own unique challenges," says Sharon Kaplan Roszia, coauthor of *Open Adoption Experience* and a national expert on adoption. "In family [or 'kinship'] adoption, everyone has two relationships to the child. The child's birth relatives are also his adoptive relatives. Adoptions within a family have 'strings attached' that reflect underlying issues in the family. Nonetheless, the child will not be confused about who his parents are as long as the adults are not confused and act accordingly."[9] Children living in kinship adoption or long-term guardianship have one set of parents in charge: the grandparents.

LEARN HOW TO BE AN ADVOCATE

Grandparents who step into the parenting role will find that the job description includes being an advocate for the child. Advocacy means that they are the mediator, petitioner, and intervener in all issues pertaining to the well-being of their child. These include school-related issues as well as medical and financial concerns. Barbara Fuller suggests that grandparents will need to learn the ins and outs of the advocacy role, such as taking notes from conversations with teachers and other professionals about school-related problems, medical situations, court proceedings, and interactions with birth parents. Grandparents will need to keep track of those conversations including the date and who they talked to about what. They will need to be assertive in contacting professionals and recontacting them if they receive an inadequate response.[10]

KNOW THAT THE CHILD YOU ARE PARENTING HAS BEEN WOUNDED

Living every day with children who have been wounded through abuse, neglect, or abandonment will present a challenge for grandparents. "These children have seen too much, heard too much, and experienced too much," says Fuller. "Grandparents are often parenting angry children with attachment disorders, sexual abuse, and multiple emotional problems. Getting support and education about the special needs of the grandchild is essential to navigating theses troubled waters."[11]

BE HONEST WITH YOUR GRANDCHILD ABOUT HIS OR HER PAST

Grandparents may be reluctant to share information about a painful episode in the family's history, an episode that may have included drug addiction, criminal history, extramarital affairs, or other potentially embarrassing scenarios. And they may be particularly reluctant to share information with a child who developmentally lacks discretion about repeating this information outside the family or asking questions of other family members.

Adoptive/guardianship grandparents have an unusually difficult balancing act on the tightrope of communication. The parties involved in the troubling circumstances are family members, people who will likely be a part of the child's future as they were his past. The principles of telling the truth to the child, however, remain the same, regardless of the difficulties involved in the task (see chapter 9). Honesty is paramount, and children are not "protected" by lies, omissions, or distortions. If grandparents try to protect the birth parents or themselves through untruths or half-truths, the children will suffer due to damaged trust, unrealistic fantasies, and anxieties about an unpredictable future.

REGULARLY DISCUSS WITH BIRTH PARENTS HOW TO HANDLE COMMUNICATION WITH THE CHILD

It is likely in grandparent guardianship/adoptions that birth parents will have some contact with the child. To ensure that information given to the child is accurate and clear, make a plan with the birth parents on strategies to explain the adoption situation, and review it regularly. Birth parents will usually be more helpful in collaboration on clear communication if they have some degree of "buy-in" about the why's and how's of interaction.

LEARN ABOUT SERVICES AND SUPPORT FOR THE CHILD AND FAMILY

Adoptive families are often eligible for adoption subsidies—financial aid for families caring for children with special needs. When family members adopt formally, they too are eligible for these subsidies. Adoptive families should contact their local child protective services agency to learn more about the financial support available to them and their children. A Medicaid card to cover health-care expenses for the child may be a part of the adoption subsidy. A website—www.gu.org—provides information on these programs.

When family members are raising relatives' children, those children may be eligible for Temporary Assistance to Needy Families (TANF) through the local Department of Human Services. This assistance also includes a Medicaid card. Further, the caregiving family might be licensed to serve as foster parents through a child protective services agency and receive foster care board rates to assist with the cost of raising children. Children in the care of relatives may also be eligible for Supplemental Security Income (SSI) through the Social Security Administration if that child is classified as completely disabled.

Finally, some states have developed programs for subsidized guardianship to help kinship parents who are willing but financially unable to care for children in need of placement. Under these programs, grandparents or other kinship caregivers do not have to meet state requirements for licensure as foster parents, but they receive a monthly payment for the support of the children. Kinship parents, whether or not they intend to adopt, can become licensed foster parents and obtain court-sanctioned custody in order to provide a safe, permanent home for the children.

Certainly, all the support needed by families is not financial. Kinship caregivers also need help with special educational needs, counseling, parenting children with special needs, day care, and health care. Many excellent support groups are forming for grandparents raising grandchildren, and adoptive parent support groups are a rich resource for families raising children with a wide variety of special needs. Local child protective services agencies and community mental health agencies can be contacted for more information about support groups, therapists, and resources within the community.

TAKE CARE OF YOUR OWN NEEDS

Yes, it is okay to do that! Staying emotionally, physically, and spiritually healthy are requirements for grandparents. "I am paying far more attention to my health," Paula said. "I eat better, exercise more. I think I am healthier than I have ever been. My motivation is that I need to be there for Josh. David and I take time for ourselves. We spend time with church friends and plan vacations together. Now that Josh is ten, he spends overnights at friends' homes. We really use that time for us to regroup and connect with our own friends."

VOLUNTARY REDEMPTIVE SUFFERING

Grandparents who step into parenting, not as a first choice, but because they felt it was the right decision for their grandchildren, are often inundated with questions from others: "Why are you doing this? Why would you give up your retirement years? Isn't there someone else who could do this? How about placing this child in foster care?"

There is an answer to those questions. I have seen it in the eyes of grandparents. I have seen it in what they have done. I have heard it from the voice of their heart. They live by a high principle in life. It isn't about them. It is about love.

Wrapping one's heartstrings around a grandchild is not a hard task. But willingly placing your own life aside is. However, hundreds of thousands of grandparents do so each year. Those with plans to adopt stand *voluntarily* in front of a judge and say, "We will be the parents of this child." Others who choose to provide a permanent home say to that child through their actions every day: "We will be here for you, by our free choice, because we love you."

This choice is not only voluntary. It is also *redemptive*. "Redeem" means to make up for or to restore. A grandparent's guiding light is the vision to restore to their abused, neglected, or abandoned grandchild the dignity of life that was ripped from him or her. It is a dignity that child was born to enjoy.

In addition to being voluntary and redemptive, the choice grandparents make to serve second shift also requires *suffering*. To extend your energies around the clock with no guarantee of a night's rest to care for an ill grandchild—that is suffering. To be told, "You are not my real mom and dad," and to continue to love, give, and pray for that child in spite of rejection—that is suffering. To see a grandchild recoil from your affection because of past abuse and to know that you would gladly carry the pain for him and can't—that is suffering.

Why do grandparents do this? Because they live their lives by the same principle that guided Jesus Christ—voluntary redemptive suffering. Heartfelt concern for a child is the impetus. Sacrificial love is the fuel. Undying commitment provides the staying power through all the ups and downs.

IN SUMMARY

Grandparents who are parenting their grandchildren need to be aware of the special challenges they face:

- The emotional toll
- Personal losses
- Financial pressures
- Boundary issues

They also need to know how to thrive, not just survive. As grandparents on second shift, you need to:

- Know that *you* are the parent.
- Learn how to be an advocate.
- Know that the child you are parenting has been wounded.
- Realize that your grandchild has a right to know the truth about his or her past. Be honest.
- Regularly discuss with birth parents how to handle communication with the child. Adapt these communications appropriately as the child matures.
- Learn about services and support for the child and family.
- Take care of your own needs.

questions for REFLECTION and DISCUSSION

1. What were some of the dreams you had for your child? In what specific ways have they been lost?
2. What have been some of your most difficult emotional moments?
3. What have been some of your personal losses? How have you adjusted to them?
4. What have been the financial pressures you've encountered? How did you handle them?
5. How have you learned to thrive, not just survive?
6. In what ways have you experienced voluntary redemptive suffering as a grandparent?

part three

mending the family tapestry

a consuming pain

8

HEALING THE LOSSES FROM ABORTION

> It had happened. Our seventeen-year-old daughter had experienced the fear of an unplanned pregnancy and the trauma of abortion. We never knew, at least not until she sat in the living room one evening and told us. There were no words to say to her that would erase her pain . . . and ours. All I could do was move to the couch where she was sitting and enfold her in my arms . . . and cry for all of us.
>
> CAROL, JESSICA'S MOM

ALTHOUGH SHERRY'S FAMILY had been part of church life for many years, when they learned of their daughter's pregnancy all they could think was, *This problem must be eliminated.* They had heard and agreed with the pro-life messages, but it was *their* daughter now. *Their* problem. They thought that by insisting Sherry have an abortion, she would avoid a lifetime of just scraping by—going from one low-paying job to another. They also felt that the abortion would rid them of something else: Sherry's less than desirable boyfriend. They thought the abortion would neatly and quietly take care of two problems.

Weeks following the abortion something began to happen to the once bright and happy daughter they had known. Her darkened countenance spoke of depression and despair. Right before their eyes, a devastating transformation stole from them the daughter they knew.

Six months after her abortion, Sherry learned of a support group for women who had had abortions. It was sponsored by the local pregnancy resource center in her town. Although reluctant and fearful to go, she went out of desperation. What she heard from those women resonated in her own heart and mind. They expressed anger at themselves for allowing the abortion to happen. Some were enraged at their parents for not helping them deal with the pregnancy in a different way. Some could barely speak above a whisper when they shared of their anger toward their boyfriends for failing to support and protect them.

A deep pain consumed Sherry. She had felt trapped between the demands of her parents, her boyfriend, and her unborn child. She felt powerless and unable to express her deepest needs and desires. When she felt forced to abort her child, she also felt that she aborted part of her womanhood. The loss of that child pierced the core of her identity. She was no longer the same person as before. She had failed to protect and defend her own baby.

Despite her boyfriend's erratic and abusive behavior, Sherry still held on to the relationship. His mistreatment confirmed her low self-esteem and sense of powerlessness. Moreover, she knew her parents hated him. By forcing her parents to accept him, she was unconsciously lashing back— echoing the way they had forced her to accept an unwanted abortion. This dynamic gave her a sense of control, yet Sherry was trapped in a vicious cycle in which she was punishing both herself and her parents. Her boyfriend, Jerrod, signified her connection to their aborted baby. She feared that giving him up would destroy the only bond remaining to the child whose death she still needed to grieve.[1]

Once Sherry began attending the support group she knew she needed some individual therapy. In sessions with her counselor, she began to verbalize her feelings more openly. She realized that in order to fully heal, she needed her parents to be a part of the process as well. She needed them to validate her loss and accept their responsibility for contributing to her emotional devastation. Without this recognition, their relationship could never be fully restored.

Stepping into the family counseling situation, both parents attempted to justify and defend their actions as they struggled with their daughter's experience. This resistance or inability to confront and admit emotional or spiritual pain is called denial. In this phase of treatment, denial is a powerful temptation.

Sherry's mom came to family therapy first. She listened to her daughter and expressed sorrow. With a pained expression, she persisted with the justifications: "I know you are hurting, but we thought we were doing the best thing. . . . I realize this is hard, but you must get on with your life. . . . You wanted the baby, but how would you ever pay for it? How would you finish school?" The list went on and on, robbing Sherry of the gift of fully acknowledging her loss. Her suspended feelings were then buried, becoming depression, anxiety, and self-punishment.

Sherry needed permission to grieve. Her parents had deprived her of the genuine compassion and acceptance she needed from them. They had not accepted the pregnancy, and now they could not even accept her grief. She felt utterly rejected by them.

father knows best?

Sherry's father had no idea what his daughter had sacrificed in order to please him. The night before the first family therapy session that would include them all, he called and left a message on the counselor's voice mail. "My stomach has been upset all week since I heard about this meeting," he said. "I want to do what is best for Sherry." Then his tone became more formal and forceful: "I just want you to know that this is *not* a moral issue to me. She had to have that abortion! I still think we made the right decision. If I had it to do again, I would choose the same thing. I know this is not what she wants to hear. Should I lie about it to make her feel better? Is that what I should do? Tell her I made a mistake? I cannot do that!"

Mr. Ellington entered the next morning with even fiercer determination. "Don't tell me that I have to tell her this was a mistake." The counselor responded, "I know you love your daughter very much. I know that she loves you or she never would have consented to have an abortion. But the fact remains that your daughter lost something. What she lost was a child. Her baby—your grandchild. Sherry thinks about it every day. She cries about it every night. The event is far from over for her. You need to hear how the abortion has affected her."

Mr. Ellington did not respond. With conviction, the counselor continued, "When someone dies, the worst thing another can say is 'It was for the best; it's better this way.' This does nothing to comfort and console; it only makes the person angry because you are not appreciating her loss or grief. Worse for Sherry is that you don't recognize the life that she is missing. Sherry misses her baby, a child you have not been able to acknowledge."

Eventually, Mr. Ellington agreed that he would try to listen and that maybe he had something to learn. But men are not prone to emotional "mushiness," he felt compelled to remind everyone. He honestly wished he could feel sorrow and compassion over the baby, but he could not. Nevertheless, he would listen if it would help his daughter.

listening and taking responsibility

When Mr. Ellington came in for the next session with Sherry and his wife, he opened the conversation with a surprising statement. "I had no right to make that choice," he said. After wrestling all week with what had been discussed in the previous session, he admitted that for the first time he realized abortion was not Sherry's choice.

The session grew very intense. Sherry expressed her anger, hurt, and feelings of rejection. She also poured out her grief about the aborted baby. Mr. Ellington began to face some things head on. He was finally able to consider the baby and to separate Jerrod from the pregnancy. To him, he said, abortion was a way to scrape out any symptom of his daughter's sexual activity and "heroically" free her from the consequences of her own actions. As these interpretations became clear to Mr. Ellington, denial could no longer sustain its powerful grip.

Suddenly, grief came upon him. He stared in disbelief, as if a light had abruptly cast shocking rays into a blackened room. His voice broke with anguish. "Oh, my baby, my sweet baby, my Sherry," he cried. "I am so sorry, I was so wrong." He pressed his face against her cheek, and the tears finally came. His tears mingled with Sherry's as they both wept. They embraced tightly as her father gently stroked his daughter's long hair. All the anger, the bitterness, the pent-up emotions, the grief, gave way. He begged for her forgiveness. Between tears and tissues, he told Sherry she would have been an incredible mother. In one beautiful moment her motherhood had been validated, and Sherry cried with relief.

In a subsequent joint session with her parents, Sherry took personal responsibility for having allowed the abortion to occur and asked her parents to do the same. This time, her parents listened without defending or rationalizing what had happened. By acknowledging Sherry's grief and sharing it with her, Mr. and Mrs. Ellington restored their relationship with their daughter. Sherry's loving and happy personality was eventually able to bloom once more. She could continue forward in her journey toward becoming a confident and capable adult.[2]

Dr. Theresa Burke, who counsels in situations just like the one above, states that this young woman's story demonstrates the complex nature of abortion. "It involves issues of family relationships, self-identity, morality, and psychological well-being." Many parents who push for their daughters to have an abortion or their sons to encourage it or who step back in a passive response to his or her thoughts about it honestly believe they are doing what is best. Rarely do they have any comprehension of the devastating psychological consequences their daughter or son or they themselves may experience.

Dr. Burke says that many families believe abortion is the quick fix needed to "turn the clock back," and allow a woman's life to go back and be the same that is was before the pregnancy. Once a woman is pregnant, Burke asserts, the choice is not simply between having a baby and not having a baby. The choice is between having a baby and having the experience of an abortion. Both are life-changing experiences. Both have significant psychological consequences.[3]

Families like Sherry's, over time face the reality of what the abortion decision really means. Many families like Sherry's suffer today in silence, telling no one of the depth of pain they are experiencing. Many families like Sherry's long for the day that they can find freedom from the tormentors of guilt, shame, and loss. They wonder if there is any road that will lead them to healing, wholeness, forgiveness, and restoration with their son or daughter, themselves, and with God.

The answer is yes: There is such a road. Dr. David Reardon, founder of the Elliot Institute, has spent the past twenty-five years researching and writing about the aftermath and healing process following an abortion. Dr. Theresa Burke and scores of others have contributed to the body of literature that addresses the journey toward healing. (Appendix II contains a list of organizations that can help address this subject.) The road to freedom and healing begins with the first step.

STEP ONE: Recognize that the road to full recovery can take time and effort.[4] "God's forgiveness can be had instantly, but sorting out your life and your feelings, overcoming the ever-present temptation to give in again to despair and doubt—these take time," says Reardon.

Mary shares her personal journey on the Rachel's Vineyard website:

When I had my abortion two and half years ago, I thought that it would be a secret that I would take to the grave with me. I never thought I would be a person to have an abortion. I always thought abortion was a personal choice, but it would never be something I could choose. I was the youngest of five. I waited to have a sexual relationship until I thought I was ready to handle everything that went along with it. I thought being out of college and having a job meant that I could handle this type of relationship. I thought if I got pregnant now that I would be financially and emotionally ready to deal with a child. I didn't plan on the man I was with walking out on me, making it the scariest time of my life. When he walked out I was five weeks pregnant. I have never felt so alone and scared.

I had an abortion because I was afraid, ignorant, and alone and confused. That one cold day in February changed the rest of my life. My life will never be the same. It has since been a life filled with guilt and shame. There was a sense of worthlessness and an emptiness that I wondered would ever go away. On the outside, life had gone on as normal, but on the inside everything had changed forever. I thought I could never truly enjoy anything anymore because I knew someone who was supposed to share it with me was gone. My daughter is gone because of my choice to abort. My choice took away a lot more than what could have been a beautiful child; it also took a large part of me.

I think of my whole life in terms of before and after the abortion. Although I was not perfect before the abortion, I at least knew I could change the things I did not like about myself. Now I hate what I have done and there is nothing I can do to change it. It was my painful secret that very few people until now knew about. I have to hide a whole part of me from my family, friends, and world. It is a hard thing to explain to your family and friends why you can't stand the holidays or your job as a preschool teacher because you don't have the daughter you never knew to share it with. They don't know she ever existed so how can they understand my emptiness.

I am happy to say that I am slowly recovering with the help of God and the good friends He has blessed me with. I am now on the long road to recreating myself and may even like myself again. It is amazing that my daughter who never even took a breath on this earth could have such an effect on my life.

I was scared to death to attend a Rachel's Vineyard retreat. I was so leery about attending that I made my friend drop me off and take my car so that I wouldn't be able to leave if I wanted to. What I experienced that weekend is hard to put into words. I went through so many different feelings in three short days, but I did not go through anything alone that weekend. There was always someone there with a hug or the words I needed to hear. We spent most of the weekend sharing stories, praying, and listening to the healing words of others.

The most wonderful thing happened on Saturday night during one of the spiritual exercises. I was able to see my daughter,

Colleen Malika, in heaven with Jesus. I finally understood that she did not hate me. Knowing this took a great weight off of me and opened the door to forgiving myself. This allows a space in my heart for hope to grow.[5]

STEP TWO: Recognize that it is normal and good to mourn the loss of a loved one. Just as mourning the loss of a parent or spouse takes time, so does mourning the loss of an aborted child/grandchild.[6]

In the case of abortion, the mourning process is often cut short and never completed because of denial or feelings of guilt. Healing can begin when people recognize how they have blocked the emotions they have regarding the abortion choice made in their family. They must courageously allow the mourning process to unfold in order to get back on track. Accepting their grief as normal rather than something that must be covered up or pushed away is critical. The pain of the loss will fade as true healing progresses.

Many people experiencing abortion loss have managed to bury their emotions for years. They play what Dr. Burke calls "mind games." Those mind games or defense mechanisms come at a high price emotionally and psychologically. In their outstanding book, *Forbidden Grief,* Burke and Reardon identify the most common defense mechanisms.[7]

SUPPRESSION

Eighteen-year-old Carolyn realized that she was pregnant just as she was beginning the second semester of her senior year of high school. Knowing that this pregnancy would destroy any hopes for college, she quietly had an abortion, telling only one close friend. For weeks following that experience, Carolyn was depressed, had bouts of rage toward family members, and was obsessed with thoughts of the abortion.

With senior exams looming over her, Carolyn forced herself to push all thoughts of the abortion out of her mind. She suppressed all thoughts and feelings about the haunting experience. Suppression became a shadowing companion that followed her through college and into her marriage.

REPRESSION

Repression is a form of selective amnesia. "It is the complete blocking out of an intolerable memory, thought, or emotion from the conscious mind," wrote Burke and Reardon.[8] Often, due to the trauma of the abortion experience, a woman has little or no memory of the details of the event. While the mind may not remember it, however, her body does.

Julia's abortion is an experience that she knows she had, but she has no conscious memory of even going to the abortion clinic. She avoids baby showers or any other activity where young children will be in attendance. If she is forced to attend she is overcome with nausea and has to leave. "Her attacks of nausea," wrote Burke and Reardon, "were like the sudden outbursts of a vigilant watchdog patrolling the edge of her consciousness, ready to repel any effort to approach her forbidden memory."[9]

RATIONALIZATION

Rationalization entails making excuses for mistakes, judgments, or failures. It generally involves a manipulative skill of distorting facts, events, or experiences. It is a skill that enables the person to maneuver successfully through false logic and inaccurate explanations. Rationalization can be a successful tool for a parent who doesn't want to face the reality of abortion or a grandparent who demanded it or stood passively by and let it happen.

Roger, angered by his teen daughter's pregnancy, insisted on an abortion. Following the procedure, his daughter attempted suicide on two different occasions. All Roger could say was that the abortion was a good choice and now his daughter could go on to college. Rationalization kept this father from stepping into the emotional dark hole where his daughter now lived.

Dr. Burke points out that defense mechanisms are pitfalls to freedom because they require a great deal of emotional energy to maintain, can distort one's perception of reality, do not filter out emotional pain, and do not cleanse people of negative experiences.[10]

In a powerful article entitled "Men and Abortion, Grief and Healing" Dr. Wayne Brauning, founder of Men's Abortion Recovery Center (MARC) in

Coatsville, Pennsylvania, offers words of strength to those who walk through the grief to healing and restoration. His words apply to all who have participated in or been touched by abortion.

Grieving for an aborted baby is different from the loss of any other loved one. Abortion is not part of any natural process like miscarriage. It is not a mysterious disappearance. It is the deliberate act of taking the life of a defenseless person.

Participating in an abortion always produces real guilt before God in the person who is responsible for the decision to take the life of the child. Men have told me that they knew they were guilty of getting the woman pregnant, of pressuring her to get an abortion, or of not coming to the rescue of the child.

Abortion also produces anger—anger at oneself for participating in the abortion, anger at others for putting on the pressure, anger at the circumstances, or anger at God for permitting it to happen in the first place. When a woman decides to abort against the desires of her child's father, the man has no legal power to protect his child. It is common for such a man to be filled with rage at the mother and others who destroyed his child.

Genuine grieving cannot happen while guilt or anger dominates our hearts. Before the grieving can begin, you must handle your personal guilt before God and others and your anger toward the persons who made the decision and toward the circumstances in which it was made.

God alone can lift the dreadful monster of guilt for participating in an abortion. In Jesus Christ, who died for sinners, God says to those who are guilty: "Come to me, all who are weary and burdened, and I will give you rest." Put yourself into His hands and through His forgiveness of your sins, He will begin to heal you so that you can find ways to make restitution for this sin. Then a genuine peace will begin to fill your heart.

Jesus is also the solution to anger. Once He enters your heart,

He will begin to transform your anger so that you can generously forgive others, as He does, and rebuild relationships with those you want to love.

Genuine grieving can now begin. First, you will grieve for the little person, whose potential you will never see fulfilled, who will never have a chance to frolic in the snow or sun or blow out her birthday candles. (An appropriate memorial service can help you begin this lifelong process of letting her go.) Then you will grieve for yourself, that your baby will never hug you, never learn the Lord's Prayer from your lips, never grow up and send you birthday cards. You will also grieve for your loved ones: your parents who will not know their grandchild, your other children who will miss the companionship of their sibling, and for the Church which is missing one person whose gifts could have been used for God's great works.

Grieve my friend, grieve! Don't hold back. The reason for this sorrow is genuine and profound. Don't try to explain it away by analyzing it. Simply let it out. And do not be afraid to share your burden with a Christian brother. You will grieve over and over again, but after a time, your walk with Christ will allow you to "cast your burden on Him and He will sustain you."

Go in His peace, carrying it as a pearl of great price to someone else who is suffering so they too may find rest in Him, and in His peace, become free to serve![11]

STEP THREE: Recognize that you are not alone. Other families have made these same decisions. Reach out for help.[12]

Some of those families attend the same church as you do. Their experiences and understanding can be of enormous help. The words of those whom God has touched, forgiven, and restored have incredible healing power.

Vicki Thorn, founder and director of the National Office of Post-Abortion Reconciliation and Healing, comments on the power of support. "A number of years ago," she says, "no woman anywhere would be talking about their abortion experience. They and their families were walking wounded. In the past few years women have started finding each other, identifying with each other, and saying abortion hurts women."[13]

There is power in reaching out for help, Thorn says. "Part of the pain of abortion is the shame wound because abortion goes against the essence of who we are as women. Society says there are no consequences to abortion, so the woman and her family who participated are increasingly isolated. If you are the grandmother and your daughter had an abortion, who can you talk to?"

This isolation, Thorn says, contributes to the dysfunctional ways people attempt to cope with abortion loss. "I have seen it so many, many times. Isolated women form surface relationships. They lose intimate friends. They have more than one abortion because they have allowed themselves to have meaningless sexual encounters."

The power in reaching out for support comes in the form of meaningful connection. "When you hear others speak of their grief," Thorn says, "it gives you permission to be in the place you are."

STEP FOUR: Extend forgiveness to yourself and to others. God does not want you to live a lifetime in mourning.[14]

As grandparents of an aborted child, you may be experiencing a consuming pain. That pain may be the result of the fact that you now know that as a result of your pressure or indecision, your daughter or son chose abortion. You know that rationalization and all the reasons you had for pushing for the abortion mock the heartache and pain and anger you feel at yourself, perhaps a spouse, your daughter or son.

In his book *The Jericho Plan: Breaking Down the Walls Which Prevent Post-Abortion Healing,* Dr. David Reardon shares something that can address your greatest need. It is about facing the reality of abortion *and* the reality of God's immeasurable ability to extend grace and forgiveness to your child, to you, and to others involved in the abortion.

"But my child did not rise from the dead," a post-aborted woman complains. "She is truly dead, and I am guilty of her death." But to such a woman I would respond that this is another example of her guilt being twisted into despair.

Death is an experience, not a state of being. For "He is not the God of the dead but of the living; for all live to Him" (Luke 20:38). When your child was killed by abortion, he or she experienced death. But your child is not dead in the sense of destroyed. Your child, like us all, is immortal. Death cannot keep her down. C. S. Lewis explains it well when he writes, "There are no ordinary people. You have never talked to a mere mortal. Nations, cultures, arts, civilization—these are mortal, and their life is to ours as the life of a gnat. But it is immortals whom we joke with, work with, marry, snub and exploit—immortal horrors or everlasting splendors." Damned or glorified, all people live on (Matthew 25:46).

Therefore, like Christ, your child lives. Your guilt can be removed precisely because God has already preserved your child from destruction. He lives! She lives! They all live in Him!

Remember, your abortion was a result of your failure to trust God. In giving you that pregnancy, God was giving you the opportunity to love. But you rejected this gift because you did not trust God's plan for you. This lack of trust and obedience is at the root of all sin, yours and mine. So it is only right that the reparation for abortion is found not by clinging to guilt and despair, but by trusting in God's love. You failed once in rejecting His gift of a new life. But now He has a new plan for you, a second gift that He passionately desires for you—the gift of His forgiveness, the birth and renewal of your spirit.

To refuse God's mercy is to refuse His love. Don't insult Him by refusing His forgiveness. Accept God's forgiveness, not because you deserve it, but so that God can use you as an instrument for showing the abundant glory of His mercy. Accepting the gift of God's forgiveness is actually a humble thing to do. It is your first step toward obedience which is rooted in faith. It is your only escape from the tar pit of despair.[15]

What if you as a grandparent learned of your child's abortion only after it happened? What about your hurt, anger, and grave disappointment? Can there be—should there be—forgiveness? In a pamphlet entitled, "Your

Daughter's Abortion and You," distributed by Focus on the Family, the author points out three key things to remember as you process this news.

1. Realize your daughter may have had the abortion to spare you the disgrace of her pregnancy or because she did not want to admit her sexual activity to you.

2. Understand your daughter may not have considered that abortion kills an unborn baby. She listened to the "lies" of those people who were too willing to "help" her fix the problem. Now she may hurt far more than you realize.

3. Comfort your daughter as she experiences the spiritual and emotional turmoil that is a consequence of her abortion decision. You lost a grandchild, but your daughter must live the rest of her life knowing she participated in the death of her own unborn baby. Cry with her. Find support together with those who have also been there.[16]

Forgive others—your daughter, your son, or their friends and advisors who participated in this decision. Recognize that they, too, may have acted out of ignorance, fear, or petty human selfishness. If possible, let them know that you forgive them.

STEP FIVE: Recognize that your aborted grandchildren do exist. Give them over to the care of God, their heavenly Father, and the true Parent of us all.[17]
Trust that they are loved, happy, and well cared for. Do not try to hold onto them by prolonging your grief. Hold them in your heart by sharing their happiness in heaven.

Thus says the LORD:
"A voice was heard in Ramah,
Lamentation and bitter weeping,
Rachel weeping for her children,
Refusing to be comforted for her children,
Because they are no more."

Thus says the LORD:
> "Refrain your voice from weeping,
> And your eyes from tears;
> For your work shall be rewarded, says the LORD,
> And they shall come back from the land of the enemy.
> There is hope in your future, says the LORD,
> That your children shall come back to their own border."

(Jeremiah 31:15-17)

God gives hope for healing as young women, men, and their families move toward reconciliation with themselves and with their unborn child. Vicki Thorn, in ministering to post-abortive families for over fifteen years, gently suggests the following steps toward closure.[18]

ACKNOWLEDGE THE REALITY OF THE LOSS.

Your daughter may have always dreamed of being a mother. Her reasons for choosing the abortion or for your choosing it for her may have made sense at the time. However, now that pregnancy, baby, and motherhood have been rejected. She sacrificed an identity that was important to her. That unique loss must be recognized.

NAME THE BABY.

Grandparents need to get a handle on who this lost baby is. One mother recently shared the story that her daughter, in spite of her offers of support, had an abortion—of a little girl. The day before the abortion, the mother got a red rose and wrapped it in a baby blanket. She named the granddaughter she would never know this side of heaven. "Rose," she called her. In this way, she felt she was able to recognize the child's uniqueness as the person she was.

WRITE A LETTER TO THE BABY.

Say all the things you need to say. This may include asking the baby's forgiveness or forgiving the baby for coming at an inconvenient time. Also consider writing an *unmailed* letter to your daughter or son, expressing your feelings about them as well.

RITUALIZE YOUR LOSS.

Use symbolic objects such as baby pictures, clothing, or whatever is meaningful to you in making your grandchild more concrete. Consider performing a ritual of letting go, such as a private funeral rite. You may want to purchase something to keep, such as a locket or a tree, to remind you of the child. Writing songs and poems or producing artwork are also helpful parts of the healing ritual for some.[19]

Some families have planted rose gardens or trees, placed a statue of an angel and child together. One family had the child's name engraved on the headstone of the child's great-grandmother. It gave them a concrete way to mark the passage of this child, ever so briefly, through their lives.

IN SUMMARY

When a physical wound begins to heal, it can be painful and irritating. But to completely heal, one must endure that pain. The same holds true for emotional and spiritual healing—it takes walking through the flames of sorrow and repentance to find healing and freedom on the other side. Healing from abortion requires that these steps be taken:

- Recognize that the road to full recovery can take time and effort.
- Recognize that it is normal and good to mourn the loss of a loved one. Just as mourning the loss of a parent or spouse takes time, so does mourning the loss of an aborted child or grandchild.
- Recognize that you are not alone. Other families have made these same decisions. Reach out for help.
- Extend forgiveness to yourself and to others. God does not want you to live a lifetime in mourning.
- Recognize that your aborted grandchildren do exist. Give them over to the care of God, their heavenly Father, and the true Parent of us all.

questions for REFLECTION and DISCUSSION[20]

1. Do you find yourself struggling to turn off the feelings and thoughts regarding the abortion experience?
2. Do you refuse to allow any conversation with your son or daughter regarding the experience?
3. Do you have "anniversary reactions" at certain times of the year, such as the expected due date of your grandchild or the abortion anniversary?
4. Do you find yourself obsessing with rationalizations as to why you encouraged your daughter or son to abort their baby or why you stood idly by and let it happen?
5. Have you struggled with feelings of anger and unforgiveness toward your son or daughter for allowing this entire situation to occur (the pregnancy) which resulted in the abortion?
6. Have you shut down emotionally over this abortion, not allowing any feelings about it to rise to the surface?
7. Do you find yourself keeping busy with career or other pursuits or encourage your daughter or son to do so to prove the abortion decision was the right one?
8. Do you tend to see your daughter or son and yourself in a "pre-abortion" and "post-abortion" time frame?
9. How would you describe your relationship with or concept of God since the abortion occurred?

nothing but the truth

9

SHEDDING SECRETS AND COMMUNICATING TO THE CHILD

To keep a secret from someone is to block information or evidence from reaching that person and to do so intentionally. It is a purposeful act. To keep a secret is to make a value judgment, for whatever reason, that it is not that person's right to process the secret. To keep a secret requires a complicated maze of family communication manipulated by concealment, disguises, camouflage, whispers, silence, or lies.

MARY WATKINS AND SUSAN FISHER
AUTHORS OF *TALKING WITH YOUNG CHILDREN ABOUT ADOPTION*

"WHEN YOU HOLD your grandson for the very first time, you will experience a whole new level of love." That is what my friends told me. And that is exactly what happened. Micah, a bright, curious, never-still-for-a-moment kind of little boy is now five (*and* one-half, as he frequently reminds me!). It hardly seems possible. We have had many joyous moments watching his first steps, hearing his first words, seeing his first flip off a diving board (at age three!), and cheering at his first hit at a T-ball game.

However, now that Micah is growing older, we know that the love we felt for him in those precious first moments and a love that grows deeper every day will require something important from all of us who touch his life. That something is critical to his understanding. That something is fragile, and perhaps it will be painful. Yet that something is freeing. It is the truth. Micah deserves full accounting of his biological heritage. He needs to know the truth about who his birth father is and, to the degree we understand and know, why his birth father isn't around.

As I thought of the hundreds of thousands of grandparents just like us who have a relationship with their grandchild directly (their adult child is parenting or they are) or indirectly (through a level of openness in adoption), I also had to think of the children whose lives they touch. I asked myself one question concerning the children, like Micah, who will need to know their whole history, the whole truth. That question was, "What would it be like if . . . ?"

What would it be like if you were Laurie? When Laurie was fifteen, she was sitting around a pool at a family reunion when she overheard her aunts talking about her father, John. They were reminiscing about the day he adopted Laurie. Adopted! She had never heard the word in relation to herself. Laurie slipped away from the crowd and confronted her parents in their motel room. Yes, it was true. Everyone knew—her aunts, her uncles, and of course, her grandparents. They all knew that the man Laurie believed to be her biological father was not. Laurie's mom had been a single mom with a three-month-old when she met her future husband. John adopted Laurie just after her first birthday. Family members all agreed that she would never really need to know. But Laurie kept asking, "Why didn't you tell me the truth?"

What would it be like if you were Jason? On a rainy afternoon, Jason was cleaning out the attic and stumbled across the family cedar chest. He had really never looked in it, but thought, why not? He opened an old shoebox full of pictures. A couple of photos grabbed his attention and confused him. They were of his sister, Susan, at age sixteen, holding him when he was a newborn. However, on the back of the picture it said "Jason and his mother. Two days old." How could this be? Later that evening, sitting around the dining room, Jason pushed his family for the truth. He learned that night that Susan, his sister, was actually his birth mother. His grandparents adopted him and raised him as their birth son. They thought it would be less confusing to him never to tell him. Jason kept asking, "Why didn't you tell me the truth?"

Why do families keep secrets? They choose to withhold information for a variety of reasons. This chapter is written not only for grandparents, but is also important information that can be passed on to their adult children who are parenting or to the adoptive parents of their grandchild.

the tool of secrecy

Laurie's parents and grandparents did not mean to harm her in any way when they withheld the truth about John's status as her adoptive father. They all truly believed it was the right thing to do. Her family, like many families in similar scenarios, used the tool of secrecy *to protect*.[1]

Jason's grandparents made a decision to keep the truth from him for another reason. Their daughter's unplanned pregnancy was very difficult for them. Shortly after Jason's birth, they moved to a new town, and because they adopted him they felt they didn't need to tell anyone he was their grandchild. Jason's family, like many families in similar scenarios, used the tool of secrecy *to hide a sense of shame*.[2] Such shame leaves the shielded one feeling like a failure, defective, and powerless.

Joyce and Kelly had been close friends for a number of years. They shared hurts, hopes, dreams—just about everything. Yet, there was a missing piece that Joyce had never shared. While they were finishing lunch one afternoon, Joyce quietly said, "Kelly, I need to tell you something that I have not shared with anyone since we moved here. When I was seventeen, I had a baby. Jeremy is that baby. When he was just over a year old, I met Kevin and we married.

"My parents felt that Jeremy didn't need to know that Kevin is not his biological father. I agreed with them, but now I'm not sure. What is so big for me is that if he finds out, everyone will know. I couldn't bear it if people at church knew." Joyce, like many young women in this situation, used the tool of secrecy *to guard her reputation and public image*.[3]

Sixteen-year-old Vickie was adopted by her grandparents when she was two years old. She had been severely neglected, often left an entire day by herself. It was her grandfather, her father's father, who contacted the local children services agency begging for intervention. Vickie was placed with her paternal grandparents and she grew up knowing she was adopted, but not that her adoptive parents were her birth grandparents. Believing they were doing the best thing, her parents thought that the less said about Vickie's past the better. "If it's not talked about, it will be forgotten," they reasoned. The entire family maintained the attitude that bad things belong buried in the past. Vickie's family, like many families, used the tool of secrecy *to forget about the past.*[4]

Even when people have the best intentions, keeping secrets can negatively impact a family. Secrets have power over family members because nobody talks about them, and yet a few influential ones know the truth. A little lie is told. A little bit of a cover-up is relayed. A secret is born. It gains more power. There is often a cost—a high cost.

the high cost of keeping secrets

Secrets are powerful. They have the ability to distort reality, undermine trust, and destroy intimacy. They can destroy authenticity and create exclusion and division.

"I felt stupid and foolish when I found out that the man who raised me was not my father," Jonathan said. "Before the secret came out, I was always so proud to hear, 'You really look like your father.' 'Peas off the same pod,' my grandmother would say. The truth is, it isn't the same 'pod,' not even close. What it feels like to me is that everyone, including my grandmother, was lying to me. What I thought was reality, wasn't."

When Teresa found out that her older brother was adopted, it impacted her relationship with her mother. "My mother and I had always been close. We talked a lot about pretty deep things. I felt that I could tell her everything. When I was seventeen, she told me the family secret—that my father was not my brother's father. My dad had adopted him when he and my mother got married. I think I was angrier that they had kept the truth from Rich than from me. It was his life. He deserved to know the truth. Over time, I found myself sharing less and less with my mother, guarding what I did tell her and always wondering in the back of my mind, *What else has she not told us?*"

In secret-keeping families, another issue emerges: the creation of the family mask. According to Michael and Julie Mask, the authors of *Family Secrets*, what the family members appear to be to one another on the outside is not what is true on the inside. In secret-keeping families, a sense of authenticity is lost.

"Living with secrets," the Masks say, "means remaining entangled in a web of deception, even if the motive is pure and protective. Deception is so destructive that it breaks trust and breeds confusion. When the truth is kept secret, then corresponding emotions are denied or repressed, and defense mechanisms rise to take their place. When children are told, 'Don't think, don't ask, don't see, don't feel,' they lose their sense of what is real."[5]

One birth grandfather, Roger, said, "We made the decision to take on the 'pretending to be her parents' role with Katherine when she came to us as a six-month-old. We didn't call it that, but that is exactly what it was. Although we were really her grandparents, at forty we were still young enough to be her parents. The older she got, the tighter the mask of pretending became. When she was eleven, we told her the truth. No more masks in our household—no more lies."

Keeping a secret divides family members into exclusive clubs—those who know it and those who do not. Secrecy controls many arenas of the secret keeper's life. To keep the secret, the secret keeper must carefully guard all communication with others close to him. This defense mode often leads to distance, anxiety, and awkwardness in relationships with others.[6]

One birth mother said, "I finally realized that it was crucial for Kevin to understand the truth about who his biological father was and who John, my husband, was to him. There came a point where I had to tell him, and when I did it felt like a weight had been lifted from me. I worried whenever we were with family members that somehow the 'secret' would slip out. Now that he knows the whole story, we have a newfound emotional freedom in our family."

If secrecy or sharing only half-truths in a family has the potential to be so destructive, what do families need to know about telling the truth?

eight principles of truth telling

In families touched by unplanned pregnancies, the truth is lived out in a variety of ways. Sometimes birth parents choose an open adoption. The truth that must be shared explains who the birth parents and birth grandparents are to the child. Sometimes a young mother, like our daughter, chooses to parent her child. The truth that must be shared over time with Micah revolves around the fact that Kristy married, and the man raising him is not his biological father. When grandparents legally step into the position of parents, the truth must be shared in those cases as well.

In all these scenarios, grandparents can play a key role because they have a relationship with their grandchild. They need to understand that their grandchild needs and deserves a full accounting of the story of his or her life. The following principles are guidelines that will prove helpful in telling the truth.[7]

PRINCIPLE ONE: *Encourage your adult child who is parenting your grandchild to initiate conversation about the life circumstances the child needs to know.*

Parents faced with the need to tell their child information that is crucial to his or her understanding of personal identity and history often handle these discussions in the same way they handle conversations about sex. They believe they should wait until the child asks questions and answer only the questions asked by the child. As a grandparent, you can explain that this strategy is not helpful in assuring that children understand their stories. You can also suggest fun and creative ways for your child to communicate the truth to your grandchild.

One helpful tool is storytelling. The Thanksgiving before Micah turned three, our family was sitting around in our living room talking about Micah's birth and cute antics from his earlier days. Kristy's husband, Rick, mentioned that it grieved him not to have known this precious little guy from the very beginning.

A week after that family event, God prompted me to create a picture storybook that would have two purposes: first, to meet Rick's need of knowing more about Micah and second, to give Kristy and Rick a tool they could use to talk with their son about the things he needed to know. I titled the picture book, *Daddy, Before I Knew You.* Even two years later, I hear occasionally that Rick and Kristy get that book out and read it to Micah. The older he becomes, of course, the greater his understanding will be. But for now, his parents are laying the groundwork for openness and truth throughout his lifetime.

Just recently, while riding in the car, Micah asked Rick out of the blue what "adopted" means. Rick, at first caught off guard by the question that seemed to come from nowhere, simply told Micah that when he met his mommy, both of them had the last name of Schooler. "I married Mommy so she would be a Matheson. I adopted you so you would be a Matheson, too!" Throughout their home are pictures of Rick and Kristy's wedding, which of course, includes Micah. There are also pictures of the day that Rick formally adopted him. These will be great tools for continued storytelling.

Another young lady, Meg, who began parenting as a single mother, faces the same challenge as Kristy. She is now married, and together she and her husband keep the truth in front of their son. "Basically, what I have told Cade is that his father's name is Steven Robert Brown," Meg said. "He looks a lot like his dad—same hair color, same eyes, same teeth, same build, and I have told him that. I explained to him that his dad was a nuclear engineering major and that when we met it was like meeting your best friend for the first time. We used to have a lot of fun together. I told him that one time, as we were driving down the street, a song came on the radio, and Steve yelled, 'Pull over, hurry!' I did, and he came over to my side of the car and opened my door and turned up the radio and started dancing with me. Just a funny moment, but I think it's important to let Cade know about his dad's personality."

Steve was not involved with Cade at all. After meeting his son once, Steve disappeared and Meg has never heard from him again. In one conversation, Meg explained Cade's father's absence to him by saying that some people just aren't ready to be parents. "I told Cade that he needn't let it upset him, as it wasn't about anything he had done. I just explained that it was his father's loss because he would never be able to get to know the child that I considered to be the most beautiful being on the face of the planet. I also told him that maybe we could find Steve if he wanted to one day, but that choice would be up to him, and there were no guarantees."

Continuing, Meg shared, "I feel it's important to let Cade know that my husband Jarred *chose* him. He will feel abandoned by Steve and this is a feeling I understand, having felt the same way about my own father. I talk to Cade about my own experiences with my father in the hopes that he will see the correlation and feel he can confide in me about it."

Meg says that there is no easy way to communicate openly and honestly with her son, but she feels that she would do him a great injustice if she didn't. "I chose to tell him the truth and pick up the pieces later," Meg says. "It's a fine line I walk because I have to be so careful in regard to what I say about Steve. I don't want Cade to hate him, yet I have to be honest and let my son find his own way. My primary goal is to not let him think that he had any fault in the situation, and to help him understand that his self-worth is not based upon one person's actions or inactions."

It is important that grandparents and parents are in agreement about how the story of the child's life will be communicated. Although Micah is still very young, I do anticipate the day when he will ask me questions. I need to know what his parents have said and what they want communicated to him, age appropriately.

In working with other families facing these issues, I have found that there are a number of other helpful ways to introduce the topic within the parent and grandparent household and nurture the child's self-esteem at the same time:

- When a program or movie with a similar life theme is on television or at the theater, watch the program or film with the child. Draw parallels and contrasts between the situation in the program and the child's own story. Use this conversation as a springboard to elicit additional questions.
- Use key times of the year (often birthdays, Mother's Day, holidays, anniversaries of the placement) to discuss the issues. For example, an adoptive grandparent could say, "I always think about your birth mother on Mother's Day (or Father's Day). I'm sure she is thinking about you today too. Would you like to make a card for her and keep it in a special scrapbook?"
- Comment on positive characteristics about the child and talk about from whom he or she inherited these traits. For example, a parenting grandparent might say: "You have such beautiful long

eyelashes. They are just like your birth mother's eyelashes. Next time she is here, look at her eyes. You will see." Or, "You are so good at drawing (music, soccer, math)! Did you know that your birth father was good at music and sports, too?"

• Comment on the child's accomplishments, including the absent birth parent in your own expressions of pride. "What a great job!" an adoptive parent or grandparent might say. "Your birth parents would be as proud of you today as we are!"

PRINCIPLE TWO: Never lie to a child about the past or a birth family member.
Lying about a child's birth parents or history creates serious trust fissures. When the truth is revealed in the future due to a slip by either the adoptive parent or extended family, or an accidental discovery of adoption-related documents, a serious rift in the parent-child relationship occurs—a rift that is difficult to repair with an apology or explanation. What began as "protection" of the relationship with the child can become a termination of trust and intimacy in that relationship.

On Tom's twelfth birthday, his mother showed him a picture of a man he had never seen. "This is your birth father," she told Tom. Until that time, Tom had not known that his dad was not biologically related to him. His mother told him that she felt Tom was "old enough to know," but admonished, "don't ever let your father learn that you know about this. It would hurt him terribly." For the rest of his mother's life, and long into his own adulthood, Tom had difficulty trusting his mother.

PRINCIPLE THREE: Allow a child to be angry toward a birth family member without joining in.
Many of us have experienced feeling enraged when someone outside our family criticized one of our family members, even when that relative drove us absolutely crazy! As grandparents who initially did have a lot of anger regarding their grandchild's absentee birth father, David and I needed to realize how easy it was to communicate that anger to Micah. And that was not a healthy thing for us to do, for Micah's sake.

Micah will have some feelings about his birth father in the future. He should be allowed to express both positive and negative feelings about birth family members without us or other family members echoing the negative sentiments. Many children who are caught up in multiple family systems (stepchildren, foster children, and adopted children) find themselves torn by divided loyalties. If members of any of those family systems berate other involved families, the child's conflict is greatly intensified.

Refusal to join the child's anger can be an easy concept to grasp but a difficult task to accomplish. After all, grandparents *are* usually angry at birth parents who harmed their children through substance abuse (during and after the pregnancy), physical and sexual abuse, neglect, abandonment, or emotional maltreatment. When the child expresses anger or outrage, it can be extremely difficult to restrain oneself from sharing that outrage. The child's maltreatment is never acceptable, but the grandparents cannot allow themselves the indulgence of speaking negatively of the birth parents.

The following types of comments are acceptable and helpful to the child:

- "I'm glad that we are able to keep you safe now."
- "I can understand why you are so angry."
- "That must have been an awfully hard time for you. Is there anything I can do to help you now?"

The following types of comments are unacceptable and potentially harmful to the child:

- "If your mother had any sense in choosing boyfriends, you never would have been abused."
- "I cannot imagine how anyone could abuse or neglect a child. They must have been awful people."
- "They should lock up your parents and throw away the key. What they did to you was unforgivable."

*PRINCIPLE FOUR: Omissions are okay until age twelve. After that, all informa-
tion should be shared.*

The complete history may be too complicated or too "adult" to share with a toddler or even a school-aged child. It is sometimes in a child's best interest to learn about his history in "increments" appropriate to his developmental level. Parents (or grandparents) know their child's developmental level better than anyone. There are no rules about the right age for giving details to a child. This decision depends on the individual child's developmental level and comprehension.

Almost all teenagers, unless developmentally delayed, have the cognitive skills and sophistication to know all the details of their histories. In his article, "Talking to Your Adopted Adolescent About Adoption," Randolph Severson advises: "In response to the question, 'What do you say to an adopted teenager?', the answer is everything. Adopted people deserve to hear all the facts, all the information that concerns their own lives, their own histories. In other words, an adopted person deserves to know his or her story. So if, for whatever reason, the full story has not yet been told during childhood, it should be told during adolescence."[8]

However, because part of the job description of a teenager seems to be to challenge whatever messages come from adults, particularly from their own parents, adoptive parents are advised to share information prior to the time their child enters the argumentative, stormy stage of adolescence. Children of eleven or twelve will usually understand and accept information that an older youth might not.

"The instinct of parents who plan to share difficult information is to wait until the child is older, perhaps in their teens," writes Holly Van Gulden. "In my experience, this is not the optimum developmental time to share difficult information. Adolescents face two tasks which make processing and externalizing difficult information potentially problematic: individuation and separation. Teens are re-evaluating the question, 'Who am I?' based in part on their sense of their history to date. Teens are also preparing to leave the family nest . . . this is a critical and complex stage during which to offer new, different and negative information about the young person's heritage. Though they appear more vulnerable, younger children in middle childhood generally process negative information more easily— not without pain, confusion and some self-blame, but with less potential for internalizing self blame/shame for the actions/choices of others. Children ages 8–10 have more time to work and rework material and come to a positive sense of self before they begin to emotionally leave the family nest."[9]

PRINCIPLE FIVE: If information is negative, use a third party, such as a thera-
    pist, to relate the most troublesome details.

Because parents must be careful to avoid sharing extremely negative information about the birth family, they might choose to seek out a specialist, a therapist who is sensitive to these issues, to relay particularly negative information to the child. The old saying about "killing the messenger" applies here. In some cases, it is wise to avoid becoming the messenger!

Parents and grandparents deciding to use a third party to share especially troubling information with their child must be careful to choose their helper wisely. Not all therapists are skilled in working with blended, adoptive, or custodial families, and they may even be insensitive to the needs of the child or the parents. While parents may enlist the support of a professional in talking with their child about his or her history, they are not "off the hook." It is critically important that parents be present for the interview, for at least three reasons. First, they must provide emotional support to their child during a difficult interview. Second, they must be present in order to remember details that might be forgotten or misunderstood by the child. In fact, parents may want to audiotape the interview, with the permission of the child. The child will process different information at different stages of maturity and may greatly value the ability to replay the interview as a young adult. Finally, parents must communicate to their child, throughout the interview and after, that they have heard "the worst" about his history, and they still love him unconditionally. Their presence and consistency send a powerful message of love, support, and commitment to the child.

PRINCIPLE SIX: Don't impose value judgments on the information.

Information about a child's history may seem very negative, even horrific, to grandparents who are caring for their grandchild. But it may be interpreted quite differently by the child. As stated earlier, information about a child's history should never be changed or given to an older child with significant omissions. Facts must be presented, however, without the overlay of value judgments.

The child's feelings for, or memories of, the birth family may alter his perceptions of events. And his *need* to have positive feelings for his birth family will definitely color his perceptions. If facts are presented in a negative, judgmental fashion, the child can interpret this judgment as the adoptive family's rejection of his birth family, his origins, and, ultimately, himself. We do not have the right to judge birth parents. True understanding comes from "witnessing" without judgment or censure. Children must develop the maturity to do the same, and this "understanding without judgment" must be modeled for them by the people most important to them: the parents who raise them.

This avoidance of judgment can actually be a relief for many grandparents. Sometimes, they worry for years about the right time and the right way to present information they perceive to be extremely negative. The child, when presented with the facts, may not see the information as negative at all.

Cameron was conceived as the result of a date rape. His eighteen-year-old birth mother attempted to parent him, but after six months the devastation of what had happened consumed her and she could no longer keep Cameron. By then his grandparents (her parents) were emotionally attached to this little one and adopted him. Cameron knew who his birth mother was only through pictures, as she had distanced herself from the family. He knew his parents were also his grandparents. But he had never been told the circumstances surrounding his adoption, and as a preteen he became obsessed with curiosity about his story. His family wanted to protect him from knowing what his birth father had done, as Cameron's awareness of his own sexuality was beginning to develop. Not wanting to lie, they simply told Cameron that his birth mother had been too young to care for him. However, to Cameron this explanation just didn't fit with what he knew about his birth mother. He pressed for further explanation.

When he was finally told the actual circumstances surrounding his birth and adoption, Cameron expressed relief to learn that his mother was not a person of "loose morals." He understood that she was a victim and truly began to understand why things happened to him the way they did. His imagination had created a far worse scenario than the actual one.

PRINCIPLE SEVEN: Don't try to "fix" the pain.

All parents naturally try to protect their children from pain. However, adoptive grandparents must recognize that their child will inevitably experience some pain in the normal resolution of adoption-related grief. The only way "out" is "through." Parents should not impose unrealistic expectations upon themselves that by saying exactly the right things, all the child's pain and sadness caused by separation from the birth family will be erased.

When talking with anyone about a serious problem, particularly a loss, platitudes ("You'll have another child." "She was so old—it's better that she's no longer suffering.") are *not* helpful. Listening ears, soft shoulders, and understanding attitudes are *very* helpful. Sometimes in eagerness to take pain away from children, we instead take away the validity of their feelings. When in pain, children do not necessarily want explanations or reasoned thoughts about what has happened; they only want someone who understands and empathizes, "I know this hurts."

Beth Hall, founding codirector of PACT, an Adoption Alliance, writes that her daughter experienced a crisis when a storyteller at school talked about the importance of naming. The seven-year-old told her mother, "I don't think my birth mother really loved me. She didn't give me a name. I wanted her to give me a name." Beth, her adoptive mother responded, "I can't imagine how hard it must have been for you to realize that right in the midst of your class." Her mother did her best to listen and support—not try to fix or interpret—the grief of her child.[10] The mother did not give reasons the birth mother might have avoided naming the child ("It might have been more difficult to sign the surrender if she had given you a name.") She also did not try to make the child's pain evaporate by ignoring it or redirecting attention from it ("But you are with our family now, and we did give you a name. So it doesn't matter that your birth mother did not give you a name.").

Often the best remedy for emotional pain is the support that comes from being aware that another understands and accepts our feelings.

PRINCIPLE EIGHT: Remember that the child probably knows more than you think he does.

Memory is a powerful thing, even for very young children. One particular evening, Micah taught us about that.

His mother was getting him ready for bed as usual, but Micah was not his usual self. He finally said to his mother, "Mommy, I'm scared."

Surprised, Kristy responded, "About what?"

"Mommy, I can't remember Daddy at the other house."

What Micah was attempting to do in his mind was to revisit the apartment where he and Kristy had lived before Rick came into their lives and find Rick there. He was reaching back, trying to find a memory of his dad in that apartment, but Rick wasn't there. Kristy recognized this as an opportunity tell Micah his story again—at a four-year-old level, of course.

Sometimes adoptive parents tell others in the family about troublesome details of their child's history, and they plan to tell the child as well—but later. No time ever seems like the right time because school is starting, the dog just ran away, the child just had a fight with his best friend. So parents never get around to telling the child and someone else does. When information comes to the child from someone other than the parent, the child does not have the appropriate support of parents in integrating the information into a positive self-identity. And, unfortunately, information is sometimes shared that is not entirely accurate because it has been passed through too many "tellings."

As parents and grandparents contemplate what a child needs to know and when he needs to know it, a final foundational principle can guide them as they take the essential steps in communicating with their child. That principle, which incorporates all those discussed above, is simply this: "Let's live the truth here, as it is."

IN SUMMARY

Resisting keeping family secrets and working to keep lines of communication open is vital to family health. Using the following principles of truth telling can help you create an emotionally healthy environment in which your grandchild can grow.

- Initiate conversation about adoption.
- Never lie to a child about the past or a birth family member.
- Allow a child to express anger toward the birth family without joining in.
- Omissions are okay until age twelve. After that, all information should be shared.
- If information is negative, use a third party, such as a therapist, to relate the most troublesome details.
- Don't impose value judgments on the information.
- Don't try to "fix" the pain.
- Remember that the child probably knows more than you think he does.

questions for REFLECTION and DISCUSSION

1. What is the truthful information that must be relayed to your child or grandchild?
2. What are your greatest concerns about telling him or her the story?
3. What are some ways that you can initiate the conversation with your child or grandchild?
4. What might be the consequences of "lying" (with good intentions) to a child about his or her past?
5. What helpful tools have you identified in this chapter? How will you use them?

it is what it is

10

REBUILDING AND RESTORING YOUR FAMILY

> Our daughter's pregnancy and our journey through it created a differ-
> ent family in many ways. We believe that we are more honest with
> each other. We believe that we allow each other more room to not
> always do so well. We know we will fail and fall. Hopefully because of
> what we have experienced — God's grace — we offer a quicker,
> steadying hand to each other so that we can get up and continue to
> move forward toward what God has for us.
>
> DAVID AND JAYNE SCHOOLER, GRATEFUL GRANDPARENTS

THERE ONCE WAS an old man who lived in poverty in a small village. The only thing of great value he had was a beautiful white horse for which he was envied by all. He was also the proud father of one strong and brave son.

Through traumatic circumstances, much like Job's, he experienced the loss of his horse, then serious injury to his son, and further devastation. With each event and life-altering experience, the old man was bombarded by "commentators."

"Your horse is gone. You've been cursed with misfortune."

"Your only son has broken his legs, and in your old age you have no one to help you. Now you are poorer than ever."

To each comment, to each judgment, the man simply responded, "Why do you always draw conclusions? No one knows. All we can see is a fragment. Unless we know the whole story, how can we judge? No one is wise enough to know if these things are blessings or curses. Only God knows."[1]

When a family faces an untimely pregnancy, it feels like the fabric of the family is ripping and tearing. Dreams neatly woven into the family tapestry are abruptly torn away. Hopes carefully knitted into the child's life are shredded with the words, "I'm pregnant. She's pregnant." What often remains is a tattered family tapestry filled with gaping holes caused by bitterness, anger, shame, guilt, failure, and loss.

People may have comments about what this means for your family, for your daughter or son, for your grandchild, and for your future. The old man's perspective from the story above can speak to hurting parents today: *All anyone can see is a fragment of a whole story. Your daughter is pregnant. Your son is a partner in an unplanned pregnancy. No one is wise enough to know what this truly means. Only God knows. It is what it is— nothing more, nothing less. It is what it is.*

What the old man teaches readily applies to the journey of parents who have experienced this life-changing event within their families: God knows the whole picture. As families walk through the crisis and move cautiously through the decision-making process, what awaits them is the final turn— healing and restoration of their family. Without exception, the dozens of families who have shared their stories in this book have experienced such healing and renewal. They offer four key principles to guide grandparents toward that positive bend in the road.

ask god to show your child to you through his eyes

One of the first steps toward healing for parents is when they begin to look at their child differently. They no longer see that teen or older young adult as "the problem." They see him or her as a person *with* a problem, but loved by them and by God. Rick and Nancy asked God to help them see and hear their daughter, Sarah, from His perspective. What they all are learning about healing and restoration is changing their lives.

"Over a year ago, Sarah was an angry, hard young lady with burgundy dyed hair and a tongue ring, struggling in the midst of her second unplanned pregnancy," Nancy quietly shared. "Our daughter, raised in the church—how did it come to this? I look at her today and she is a delightful young lady. God has done so much. Part of the positive change began when I asked Him to let me see her and hear her as He does."

Nancy admits that it has been a very difficult road back to rebuilding the relationship and trusting her daughter, but a couple of things really helped her and her husband. First, Nancy offered, "I listen to her more now and step in to solve her problems less. I treat her like an adult. I simply ask myself, 'How would I want my parents to respond to me?'"

Second, Nancy says she has learned much about God's grace. "God showed me so much about my judgmental spirit. It has been very sobering. I am much more observing and not so quick to speak. One of the biggest things God has taught me about seeing her as He does is that I needed to be intentional about hearing her heart. I need to ask questions, but not pass judgment. It is easy to ask a leading question that portrays your thoughts, like, 'Do you *really* want to do that?' I am learning to step back and let Sarah be an adult, and to listen to her heart."

Rick added, "For years, I have been about 'fixing' Sarah. I think as fathers we have a tendency to do this. I had a conversation recently with a father of three young girls. 'Give me some advice about raising girls,' he asked me. 'Don't try to fix them,' I told him." When a daughter comes to her dad with a problem, Rick says, she just needs to be heard. It's typical for a father to want to jump right in to protect her and to fix the situation without really taking the time to listen to her.

Rick says he is learning to be much more direct with Sarah. "I say things to her like, 'What are you asking of me when you tell me this? Do you want me to just listen, or do you need me to help you?' Sarah, like many young women, just needs me, as her dad, to listen as she processes her concern."

keep your heart open

Something happens in the heart of a parent when it has been broken time and time again by the actions and reckless decisions of a child. What subtly occurs is a closing off to that child in such a way that the parent distances himself from the relationship. A protective wall forms that ends up isolating the hurting parent from friends and support. This happened to Rick and Nancy.

"We guarded our hearts in different ways, from friends and from family, perhaps even from God," Nancy said. "I wouldn't go out of my way to be too friendly with people as I had in the past. I simply lost my joy. We lived in a perpetual state of exhaustion as we walked through the situation with Sarah. Sometimes, I felt closer to the feet of Jesus during all of this. At other times, I was too tired to even sit there.

"In the midst of my emotional exhaustion, I put up a wall between me and my daughter. I wanted that wall up so Sarah could not hurt me again. However, we are beginning to come back to life—all of us. The Lord prompted a question in my heart that was a challenge to me: 'Are you ever going to open your heart again?' The answer I had to give was yes. I cannot love or be part of restoration inside of an enclosed fortress."

Another family experienced a walling off in a totally different situation. Emotional pain is something that all of us would like to avoid, but running from anguish is another way to close the heart and postpone healing.

Larry is the birth grandfather of twins. His daughter, Christi, made an adoption plan for her children. The last thing he wanted to do was to see and hold the babies prior to their placement into the adoptive home. "If I didn't see them or touch them, I wouldn't have to deal with it," Larry said. "My first inclination when they were born was I didn't want to hold them. I didn't want to hold them because I didn't want to bond with them. That was a self-protective reflex."

But Larry did hold his grandchildren. He realized that somewhere down the road he might regret missing the opportunity to hold them and love them. Because Larry opened his heart, he also experienced something else.

"Suddenly I could see God's hand in all that had happened," he shared. "I could see God's hand comforting me and my wife. She was one of my greatest concerns besides our daughter. He's placed all of us in situations where we've been able to have a support base throughout this experience. He's supplied us with acquaintances who have been very supportive of us through the whole process. I could finally recognize His hand moving through all of this."

realize that "tough love" may be God's tool for restoration

Jamie was eighteen years old, graduating from high school, and two months away from beginning Christian college when her parents discovered that she was sexually active. When Jack and Bonnie confronted their daughter, Jamie was angry and belligerent. Her dad told her that she had a choice to make. "She could choose to continue living the way she was and leave our home," Jack said, "or she could stop living that way and continue living at home. I explained that God was not pleased with her behavior and that He did not want the influence of that behavior in our home and around our younger son." Jamie walked out the front door that very night.

"The spiritual battle did not stop there," Jack said, "but continued and intensified over the next year or so. During that time, I had very little direct communication with Jamie. Bonnie, however, maintained an open line of communication, reminding her that we loved her and would welcome her back the moment her heart changed."

Holding this "tough" line was not easy for Bonnie. "I was torn," she said, "very torn between what I felt God was calling us to do and my feelings as Jamie's mom. What mother wants her children to lack for anything? But I kept thinking about the prodigal son. His father didn't enable him. He didn't help him stay out in the pigpen either. He simply stayed home and waited for his son to return of his own free will. Jamie chose to walk out; we didn't make that choice. All we really could do was wait."

It was during this period of time away from the family that Jamie became pregnant. For Jack and Bonnie, that didn't change how they saw God working as they prayed for restoration. "Prior to the pregnancy," Jack explained, "I relinquished Jamie to God. My prayer to Him was, 'Lord, you trusted her to me for eighteen years, and I have done the best I know how to do. I am turning her completely over to You. You take her and do whatever You need to do to accomplish Your will in her life.' For me that meant 'hands off.' When the pregnancy occurred, it didn't change anything. We had asked God to do whatever was necessary to bring our daughter back to Him. If that included Him working through her getting pregnant, fine. We just wanted her back."

While she was pregnant, Jamie told her parents that she wanted them to be a part of her baby's life. However, the lifestyle and attitude that had originally separated her from the family had not changed. Jack and Bonnie told her that of course they would love the baby, but held to their position that they would not do anything to enable her to continue living the way she was.

Their primary concern was for Jamie's long-term well-being, Bonnie explained. "It was not easy watching her suffer and struggle. It would have been easy to enable her through funding or compromise. I was never concerned for the baby's safety because I knew Jamie would take care of him, and I had also placed him totally into God's care. Jack and I had a sense that once she became a mother, Jamie would realize that her focus had been misplaced and she would be on the road home—restored to our family and to God."

Jamie's parents were right. Not long after Scotty was born, Jamie was restored to Christ and welcomed back to the family with her son. Jack and Bonnie are confident that God honored their "tough love" approach. Looking back, they feel that they also learned some key principles about life, God, and what love really means.

"We have absolutely no control over others and can only influence them through living holy lives and being obedient to God ourselves," Jack asserted. "What a limited God we serve if He depends upon our powers and abilities. The one thought that seems to keep everything in perspective for me is that there are approximately six to seven billion people in the world at this time, and God knows every one of their hearts. He knows exactly what each one of them is thinking at every given moment. I serve an all-powerful God. I didn't need to use my own abilities or powers to rescue Jamie from her chosen lifestyle. I simply needed to focus on the One who has power to do all things. All I had to do was humble myself in the presence of God Himself and trust Him to know and do what was best for our daughter."

know that your attitude is critical

In fact, says Dr. James Kennedy in his book, *Your Prodigal Child*, your attitude is everything. He suggests three critical attitudes that parents should practice during the difficult days of family healing.

First, do not focus on the child's wrongdoing, but on the child as a person. Many of us have refined a parenting art that has three components—lecturing, reminding, and threatening. If a son or daughter has been involved in sexual behavior that led to pregnancy, it simply is what it is. As parents we sometimes get stuck on the behavior. We fear that if we don't keep reminding or lecturing, we'll send the message that we condone the behavior we abhor. We may even believe that by focusing on the behavior, we can cause positive change in our child's life.

God taught Rick about this faulty thinking. "I used to think I was more interested in seeing Sarah's behavior change. However, I should have been more interested in her character changing. Sometimes we would see her modify her behavior, but the heart of the matter—her character—didn't change. Eventually we wised up and stopped focusing on her behavior, realizing that changing our daughter from the inside was God's job. Once we did that, we looked at Sarah differently."

A second critical attitude is reflected in Scripture: "Be swift to hear, slow to speak, slow to wrath" (James 1:19). Lecturing and threatening are forms of control and are often rooted in anger and feelings of powerlessness. Hope for healing in the family can be rekindled when parents monitor their words. In most cases, "less" words spoken can impact a young adult's heart more effectively than "more" words.

Finally, parents should adopt the attitude that it is fruitless to argue with their child about their ungodly behavior. Arguments and debates over a child's choices usually reap more arguments and debates. When parents allow themselves to fall into arguments about their child's behavior, the issue becomes the argument. Nothing constructive is accomplished. Dr. Jim Fay, author of *Parenting with Love and Logic*, points outs that there is power in the statement, "I love you too much to argue."[2] Using these words sends

181

a message about your attitude as a parent. You refuse to participate in a perpetual debate with your young adult child.

trust that your child wants to be restored to the family as much as you want him or her to be

Throughout this book we have focused on listening to parents—their issues and concerns. Earlier in the chapter, Nancy shared that she needed to take time to intentionally listen to her daughter's heart. That is what we are going to do: listen to the heart of our children as they faced the issues of unplanned pregnancy and the impact it had on their families.

JESSICA

I knew that when I told my parents I was pregnant, the news would be hurtful and devastating. It was another problem on top of a lot of other problems. I don't know how I allowed my life to get so messed up. I lost my way, but that was not where I really wanted to be.

Maybe part of what I was doing was an attempt to figure out who I really am. Maybe it was about testing Mom and Dad's love for me if I wasn't the "perfect" child I had always been. All the times my parents told me they loved me, even when I was the ugliest, and I acted like I didn't care, I really did. Mom kept saying to me, "We will always be here for you," and it finally sank deep into my heart. I didn't want them to give up on me . . . and they didn't!

SCOTT

I was away at school when Katie, my girlfriend, got pregnant. Since we were so far away, I didn't tell my parents. However, word got back to them from my sister's friends. By then, it was too late; Katie had already had the abortion. I couldn't face my parents. I was hurting too much. I didn't know what they would say. I didn't want to hear, "How could you?" or "We told you so," or anything like that. What I needed from them was the message that they still loved me in spite of this horrific ordeal and the mess I had made of things.

One afternoon, I walked into my dorm and Dad was sitting in the lobby. I didn't expect him or anticipate his response to me. "Scott, we need to talk," he said. "We know about everything. We want you to know that we love you. Yes, we were hurt and angry, but now we need to talk about you. There is some mending of your heart that needs to happen."

I just dropped on the couch beside him and for the first time in a very, very long time, I cried in front of my dad . . . and he cried, too.

KRISTY SCHOOLER MATHESON

I will never forget the day in late April, 1998, when life changed forever for me. Up to that point, I thought that I could do just what I wanted to do and never suffer any consequences. Those things happened to other people. Of course, that was a lie. As I stared at the positive pregnancy test, I was hit with an incredible wave of fear, and all I could think about was, *Everyone will know*.

Up to that point, I had been making a lot of bad choices. I had completely turned away from the morals and values from my childhood. Because I turned from God, I had an incredible emptiness that I tried to fill with the pleasures of this world. I thought that I could keep living like this. I thought that I could keep pretending that everything was all right.

I do not remember much about the days after I discovered I was pregnant. I do remember that I walked around in a thick fog of fear, denial, anger, and especially shame. Never in my life did I feel so alone. For days I reached out to no one because I did not want anyone to know. What added to my feelings of being alone also was that the baby's father showed no care or concern at all. Within seconds of me telling him about the pregnancy, he grew cold and angry. He blamed me for ruining his life and for inhibiting his pursuit of law school. He insisted that the only option was abortion.

Not only did he feel as if abortion were the only option, but I, in my desperation and shame, also felt like I had no other option. I believed that abortion was wrong. I had been very involved in the pro-life movement for as long as I could remember. I had written speeches in school about how abortion was wrong, and I had no problem defending this value in secular college classes. Even though I knew I was doing the wrong thing, I found the phone number for a local clinic and made an appointment. Then, finally, I confided in my older brother, Ray, who insisted on going with me.

The weather on the day of that initial appointment was so indicative of the way I was feeling inside. It was a cold, rainy day, and the darkness I felt inside was impenetrable. The abortion clinic I went to was always like I pictured them to be. There was a big steel door that could only be opened from the inside. When I arrived for my appointment, I had to yell into an intercom about the reason that I was there. The door unlocked, and I proceeded to walk in. As instructed, I sat down and waited for my name to be called. The lobby of the abortion clinic was cold and filled with women who were just as empty and scared as I was.

After what seemed like forever, my name was finally called. I turned and followed the woman, who did not even say hello. She was very cold and showed no emotion. I took another pregnancy test to confirm that I was pregnant, and she instructed me to go back out and sit in the lobby and wait for the results. After a few minutes, she came back out and showed me the results of my positive pregnancy test in the presence of all the other people sitting in the lobby. She then suggested that we should discuss some options. Ray and I followed her into a tiny room where she asked me some questions and then began telling her own story. She talked about why she had chosen abortion, and why abortion was the right thing for her. As I listened to her rationalize why abortion was a good decision for her, and why, given my current situation, it was a good option for me, I scheduled an appointment for May 18.

I left the abortion clinic feeling just as empty and sick as I had when I arrived. Ray's words to me, "You can't do this," followed me through the rest of the day. But I kept telling myself that after May 18 this nightmare would be over and life, as I knew it, would be back to normal.

For the next several weeks I continued to go through the motions of school, work, internships . . . but the dark cloud that followed me never gave way to light. I had occasional conversations with the birth father, but they were angry, accusing phone calls that led to deeper anger and feelings of helplessness.

I still kept my secret to myself. No one but my brother knew. Ray made several stops at my apartment and called me numerous times, but it was just easier to be alone. I withdrew more and more. I was jealous of the perceived normalcy in other people's lives that I no longer had.

Because I wanted to attempt to support myself as much as I could, I continued to be a server at a local restaurant despite the fact it would have been easier to completely quit everything. One Saturday morning as I was getting ready for work, I was thinking about my decision to have an abortion. As I always did, I began to rationalize about why I was making the right decision. I went through the list in my mind again: I am a senior in college; I have dreams for my life; I want to get a graduate degree; I cannot tell this to my parents; what will the church think; and, of course, I cannot bring this child into the world without a father.

As I was running through my list of reasons for what I planned to do, an amazing thing transpired. I heard from God. In the deepest part of my heart I sensed a very clear message: "This child may not have an earthly father, but he has a heavenly Father who wants this child to live." At that moment things began to change.

May 18 came and went, and I did not go to that abortion clinic. Although I knew things were not going to be easy from here, I felt good about my choice. I informed the birth father of my decision, and he became irate and irrational on the phone. I hung up and have not spoken to him since that day.

Because I was literally sick with the burden of knowing I would have to tell my parents about the pregnancy, I waited only another two days. Never before or since have I had to do anything as agonizing and heartbreaking as I had to do that Sunday night. In the first chapter, my mother wrote about their thoughts and feelings, which I am sure are almost impossible to describe. In spite of their deep hurt, however, it did not take long for them to become my biggest supporters. I often talk to young women now who have been in my situation, whose parents have not been supportive at all during the pregnancy and minimally supportive after the birth of the baby. I cannot imagine. I do not think I would be able to tell this story and the amazing things that have happened as a result had I not been blessed with the unconditional love and support I received from my parents and brother.

As I mentioned earlier, I wanted to continue with the plans I had for my life. I became involved in the local crisis pregnancy center and was linked with a one-on-one counselor, Nancy Caverlee. We discussed college, the birth father, family, church, parenting issues, and so much more. She encouraged me to stay in school and to keep things as normal as possible. I did. I was taking a heavy course load at school, I was doing a senior internship, and I continued to work as much as I could. I was very busy, and at times wanted to give up, but God sent people into my life who encouraged me every step of the way. Fellow students in my college classes would call me to make sure I came to class, and my practicum supervisor prayed and cried with me. A dear friend, Sue Ferryman, allowed me to work as a receptionist in a retirement village she managed. That was a blessing because waiting tables is very difficult when you are pregnant.

I was also blessed with a wonderful obstetrician. Dr. Evangeline Andarsio never treated me any differently because of my situation. She was extremely caring and supportive of my decisions. I could go on and on about people who showered me with love during the most difficult time in my life. I experienced them all as an earthly extension of God's love.

As the time grew nearer for my son to be born, I moved back into my parents' house. We began to set up the nursery and prepare for the birth. Both the church I grew up in and the current church where my dad was pastoring threw showers for me. I was blessed with amazing gifts and an outpouring of love.

The day came for my son to arrive. I had a short labor, and at 1:00 P.M. on December 29, 1999, Micah Benjamin arrived. He was so beautiful. All I could do was stare at him; I could not have dreamed of a more perfect child. I thanked God for him from the moment he was born.

While I finished my last quarter of college, I had a lot of help with Micah. I got my first job as a social worker in a nursing facility and worked hard to be as independent as possible. Although I did have a lot of support, it was very difficult to be a single parent. Most of my friends were single, and I felt very isolated at times. When Micah was about eighteen months old, the church where I attended began a young adult ministry.

Through that ministry, I met Rick Matheson. We dated for a short time, and became engaged. From the beginning, we both knew that God had put us together. I especially knew because of how he was with Micah. Rick was, and still is, an incredible father to Micah. Rick's parents, Rick and Annie Matheson, are incredible grandparents as well. The entire family celebrated on March 21, 2003, when Rick adopted Micah. Micah now announces proudly, "I'm a Matheson man."

My life has continued to change, and our family has continued to grow. Annalise Elizabeth was born February 19, 2003, and she is an incredible gift from God.

We continue to celebrate Micah's life every day. My family and I talk often about what a blessing Micah is, and how our life would be so empty without him. He is now a vibrant five-year-old who loves life and provides endless joy and laughter to us.

What God has done in my life is a miracle. This book is being written for that reason. We want people to know that *there is always hope.* No matter what the situation is or how complicated and impossible it may appear at the time, there is hope. God can restore. Give Him time.

IN SUMMARY

Healing and restoration in a family is God's business and occurs on His timetable. He has led families through the process so that they, in turn, can lead others. Here are the healing principles they have to share.

- Ask God to show your child to you through His eyes.
- Keep your heart open.
- Realize that "tough love" may be God's tool for restoration.
- Know that your attitude is critical.
- Trust that your child wants to be restored to the family as much as you want her or him to be.

questions for REFLECTION and DISCUSSION

1. Have you guarded your heart as it relates to seeking support from friends or loved ones?
2. Have you set up a wall of defense between you and your child?
3. Where in the healing process do you see yourself and your family?
4. Has tough love been a tool you have used? Could it be?
5. What barriers have you experienced in being restored as a family?
6. Do you think you are giving your child what he or she most needs in order to heal? How do you know?

resources for unplanned pregnancy

Bethany Christian Services
301 Eastern Ave. NE
Grand Rapids, MI 49503-1295
1-800-238-4269
http://www.bethany.org
Provides pregnancy counseling, temporary foster care, and alternative living arrangements for pregnant women and national and international adoption services. Also offers family and marital counseling and services for refugees, runaways, and homeless youth. Bethany has seventy offices across the country.

Loving and Caring
Jim and Anne Pierson
1905 Olde Homestead Lane
Lancaster, Pennsylvania 17601
717-293-3230
http://www.lovingandcaring.org
E-mail: mail@lovingandcaring.org
Loving and Caring, Inc. is a life-affirming ministry lending its support, experience, and expertise to a myriad of national and international life-affirming ministries by providing resources, training, and restoration. Their greatest desire is to inform and train these ministries, offering them spiritual and physical refreshment and renewed hope.

Birthright
1-800-550-4900
> Provides free and confidential pregnancy testing, support for pregnant women, maternity and baby clothes, parenting classes, adoption services, medical care, family counseling, and referrals for legal assistance.

Care Net
109 Carpenter Dr., Suite 100
Sterling, VA 20164
1-800-395-HELP (1-800-395-4357)
http://www.care-net.org
E-mail: carenet@juno.com
> A national network of crisis pregnancy centers that help women in need with free pregnancy tests, maternity clothes, medical and professional services, and special care for single mothers. Also offers post-abortion counseling.

Heartbeat International
Peggy Hartshorn, President
665 E. Dublin-Granville Rd., Suite 440
Columbus, OH 43229
1-888-550-7577
http://www.heartbeatinternational.org/
> An international association of pregnancy resource centers and medical clinics, maternity homes, and nonprofit adoption agencies that provide sexual integrity programs, pregnancy testing and cirsis intervention, maternity support, and healing programs for sexual trauma and post-abortion.

online resources

Abortion/Post-Abortion
> Ramah International—http://www.ramahinternational.org
> Rachel's Vineyard—http://www.rachelsvineyard.org (post-abortion)
> Project Rachel—http://www.hopeafterabortion.com (post-abortion)

Abstinence
> National Abstinence Clearinghouse—www.abstinence.net

Family
> Focus on the Family—http://www.family.org
> Family Research Council—http://www.frc.org

Fatherhood
    National Fatherhood Initiative—http://www.fatherhood.org
    Loving & Caring—http://www.lovingandcaring.org

International Pregnancy Center Support/Resource Organizations
    Heartbeat International—http://www.heartbeatinternational.org
    Life International—http://www.lifeinitiatives.org

Pregnancy Center Support/Resource Organizations
    Baptists for Life—http://www.bfl.org
    Care Net—http://www.care-net.org
    Focus on the Family Crisis Pregnancy Ministry—http://www.family.org/pregnancy
    Heartbeat International—http://www.heartbeatinternational.org
    The Heidi Group—http://www.heidigroup.org
    Sav-A-Life—http://www.savalife.org
    The National Institute of Family and Life Advocates—http://www.nifla.org
    Birth Mother Advocate—http://www.hearttoheartadoption.net
    Option Line—http://www.optionline.org
    Loving & Caring—http://www.lovingandcaring.org

Single Parenting Program Resources
    Crown Financial—http://www.crown.org/SingleParents
    Loving & Caring—http://www.lovingandcaring.org

Training Resources
    At the Center Magazine—http://www.atcmag.com
    Loving & Caring—http://www.lovingandcaring.org

resources for healing after abortion

Below is a partial list of the many organizations worldwide that offer support and counseling to those struggling with a past abortion. Many offer phone or online counseling or referral to a counselor or support group in your area.

It is important when contacting these resources or any other organization that you ask a lot of questions to make sure that you are in agreement with their philosophies and practices. The services offered by these groups are confidential and, in many cases, free.

While careful attention has been made to verify the work and credentials of the organizations below by those respected by this author, this list should not be considered an endorsement.

Rachel's Vineyard Ministries
Theresa Karminski Burke, Ph.D., and J. Kevin Burke MSS/LSW, Directors
P.O. Box 195
Bridgeport, PA 19405-0195
1-877-HOPE-4-ME (1-877-467-3463)
http://www.rachelsvineyard.org
  Offers post-abortion weekend retreats and support groups at many sites across

the U.S. and abroad. Provides leadership and clinical training seminars, conferences, publications, and resources for other healing ministries that wish to sponsor the retreats. Current retreat dates and locations are listed on the website.

Hope Alive
Dr. Philip Ney and Dr. Marie Peeters Ney
International Institute for Pregnancy Loss & Child Abuse Research & Recovery
P.O. Box 27103, Colwood Comers
Victoria, BC V9B 5S4
CANADA
250-642-1848
http://www.messengers2.com
E-mail: iiplcarr@islandnet.com
> Provides research and training for people in group counseling, as well as support for those affected by child abuse or abortion, and research and support for survivors of attempted abortion and those who have lost a sibling to abortion.

Hope Alive USA
Sonja Kvale
52 Waleny Dr.
Bella Vista, AR 72715
479-855-0072
http://www.HopeAliveUSA.org
E-mail: HopeAliveUSA@aol.com
> Group treatment program for those deeply damaged by child abuse, neglect, and pregnancy loss. Helps set up training, resources, and supervision for those desiring to become Hope Alive counselors. Provides referrals to trained counselors for those desiring the thirty-week treatment program.

The National Office of Post-Abortion Reconciliation and Healing
Vicki Thorn, Director
P.O. Box 07477
Milwaukee, WI 53207-0477
414-483-4141
1-800-5WE-CARE (national referral number)
http://www.marquette.edu/rachel
> National office of Project Rachel, a ministry of the Catholic Church composed of a network of specially trained clergy, spiritual directors, and therapists who provide compassionate care to those who are struggling with the aftermath of abortion. Provides confidential help to women and men of all faiths. For referrals to support groups and outreaches of various denominations, contact the national referral number.

Option Line
(Sponsored by Care Net and Heartbeat International)
1-800-395-HELP
http://www.optionline.org
   Trained consultants answer calls and e-mails 24 hours a day, 7 days per week, and refer callers to the closest post-abortion healing program in a pregnancy resource center.

Ramah International
Sydna Masse, Director
1776 Hudson Street
Englewood, Florida
941-473-2188
http://www.ramahinternational.org
   Seeks to bring post-abortive individuals to Christ's healing, and supports post-abortion ministry through training programs, resources, and research.

resources for men

Fathers and Brothers Ministries
350 Broadway Suite 40
Boulder, CO 80303
303-494-3282
   Provides support, counseling, and information for men who have lost children to abortion.

Loving and Caring
Jim and Anne Pierson
1905 Olde Homestead Lane
Lancaster, Pennsylvania 17601
717-293-3230
http://www.lovingandcaring.org

resources for grandparents raising grandchildren

Books

Relatives Raising Children: An Overview of Kinship Care by Joseph Crumbley (Editor). Child Welfare League of America, August 1997.

> Dr. Crumbley provides the reader with excellent descriptions of the many issues found in the growing phenomena of family members raising their grandchildren or other relative children. The authors offer an inside look from the perspectives of the child, the relative caregiver, and the parent in this difficult situation.

To Grandma's House, We—Stay: When You Have to Stop Spoiling Your Grandchildren and Start Raising Them by Sally Houtman. Studio 4 Productions, March 1999.

> This book is a timely road map that guides grandparents through unfamiliar territory by offering practical solutions to the real-life problems they'll face. The author shares compassionate wisdom and advice to lead readers through the obstacle course of emotions, conflicts, legal, and social considerations that lie ahead.

Raising Our Children's Children by Deborah Doucette-Dudman. Fairview Press, April 1997.

> Principal issues addressed are managing stress, negotiating legal hurdles, locating support, telling children their life stories, managing conflict, and creating a stable, secure, permanent setting for children whose parents cannot or will not parent.

Grandparents as Parents by Sylvie De Toledo and Deborah Edler Brown. Guilford Press, July 1995.

This book deals with the many predictable and unexpected issues grandparents may face in their relationship with the child. Those effects include the impact on the grandparents' lives, effects on other family members, getting help for a troubled child, and dealing with the child's natural parent(s). The authors also guide the reader through the maze of legal terminology of which they will need to be familiar. "This is a reference book, a character-builder, a challenge, and a friend."

Websites

http://www.aarp.org/life/grandparents—This website is a rich resource for grandparents raising grandchildren, step-grandparents, or those with visitation issues. It also addresses legal, financial, education, health, and support challenges.

http://www.grandsplace.com—This is an informative and supportive website for those grandparents who feel that they are alone in meeting the challenges of raising their grandchildren.

http://www.adoption.org/adopt/grandparents-as-parents.php—This site offers numerous other links to resources for grandparents who are raising their grandchildren.

http://www.aarp.org/confacts/money/tanf.html—This site has information on financial assistance for grandparents.

http://www.grandparentagain.com—This website offers information about education, legal support, support groups, and other organizations for grandparents raising grandchildren.

notes

INTRODUCTION

1. Anne Pierson and her husband, Jim, started Loving and Caring in 1984. Two years prior to beginning this national ministry, President Ronald Reagan mentioned their contribution to helping pregnant women as founders of The House of His Creation, a maternity home and aftercare ministry in Coatesville, Pennsylvania. The president's commendation sparked calls to the Piersons from around the nation, and these callers were the inspiration to begin the new national ministry of Loving and Caring.

CHAPTER TWO

1. Curtis Young, *The Missing Piece: Adoption Counseling in Pregnancy Resource Centers* (Washington, D.C.: Family Research Council, 2000), p. 8.
2. Linda Schindler, interview by author, April 26, 2002.

CHAPTER THREE

1. Mary Martin Mason, interview by author, June 17, 2003.
2. Anne Babb, *Ethics in American Adoption* (Westport, Conn.: Bergin & Garvey, 1999), p. 118.
3. John Ensor, interview by author, June 19, 2003.
4. Jim Pye, interview by author, June 26, 2003.
5. Jim Pye, "Fishers of Men," *At the Center* (Scepter Institute) vol. 4, no. 1, Winter, 2003, p. 8.

6. Mason interview.
7. Susan Speak, Stuart Cameron, and Rose Gilroy, "Young, Single, Non-residential: Their Involvement in Fatherhood," *Social Policy Research* (Joseph Rowntree Foundation, 1997) vol. 137.
8. Robert I. Lerman and Theodora J. Ooms, eds., *Young Unwed Fathers: Changing Roles and Emerging Policies* (Philadelphia: Temple, 1993), p. 45.
9. Lerman and Ooms, p. 45.
10. Brenda Romanchik, interview by author, June 25, 2003.
11. Archie R. Wortham, *Teen Fathers Need a Dad, Too!* (www.teendad.net).
12. Thomas Strahan, "Portraits of Post-Abortive Fathers Devastated by the Abortion Experience," *Assoc. for Interdisciplinary Research in Values and Social Change*, 7(3), Nov/Dec 1994.
13. http://www.afterabortion.org/PAR/V4/n4/MenandAbortionArticle.htm.
14. Strahan, "Portraits."
15. http://www.afterabortion.org/PAR/V4/n4/MenandAbortionArticle.htm.
16. Romanchik interview.
17. Ensor interview.
18. Pye interview.
19. Ensor interview.
20. Ensor interview.
21. Pye interview.
22. Mason interview.
23. Romanchik interview.
24. Carrie Fiasco, adoption manager, The Children's Home of Cincinnati, Ohio, interview by author, June 19, 2003.
25. Ensor interview.
26. Wortham.
27. Mason interview.
28. Pye interview.
29. Pye interview.
30. Pye interview.
31. Ensor interview.
32. Pye interview.

CHAPTER FOUR

1. Trudy Johnson, "Understanding Post-Abortion Aftermath" (Evansville, Ind.: Master's Graduate School of Divinity, 2003). Johnson is the author of the first college curriculum in post-abortion counseling.
2. Alan Guttmacher Institute, "Induced Abortion," *Facts in Brief*, January 1998.
3. Curtis Young, *The Missing Piece, Adoption Counseling in Pregnancy Resource Centers* (Washington, D.C.: Family Research Council, 2000), p. 8.
4. Dr. Charles Kenny, interview by author, August 26, 2003. Kenny & Associates, Inc. conducted IN-SIGHT interviews in St. Louis, Missouri, in 1994. The purpose of the study was to develop an in-depth understanding of the psychological

dynamics that drive the ways in which moderate, mainstream women, who morally opposed abortion, find it to be acceptable in certain circumstances.

5. Paul Swope, "Abortion: A Failure to Communicate," *First Things,* 82, April 1998, pp. 31-35.

6. Swope, p. 32.

7. Swope, p. 32.

8. Warren Williams, "Restoring Fatherhood Lost," *The Post Abortion Review,* 4(4) Fall 1996.

9. Jim Pye, "Father's Day Lost," *unpublished article.*

10. Catherine Hickem, "Understanding Why Christian Mothers Push Their Daughters Toward Abortion," *Heartlink* vol. 10, no. 2, February 2003, p. 1.

11. Hickem.

12. Hickem.

13. Dr. Theresa Burke, interview by author, April 5, 2003.

14. Deena Crandall, interview by author, May 5, 2003.

15. Burke interview.

16. Burke interview.

17. Crandall interview.

18. Burke interview.

19. Dr. Theresa Burke and Dr. David Reardon, *Forbidden Grief* (Springfield, Ill.: Acorn Books, 2002), p. 225.

20. Nancy Hird, "Abortion in the Church: The Untold Story," *Moody Magazine,* March/April 2002, pp. 45-49.

21. Hird.

22. H. L. Howe, et al., "Early Abortion and Breast Cancer Risk Among Women Under Age 40," *International Journal of Epidemiology,* 18(2):300-304 (1989); L. I. Remennick, "Induced Abortion as a Cancer Risk Factor: A Review of Epidemiological Evidence," *Journal of Epidemiological Community Health* (1990); M.C. Pike, "Oral Contraceptive Use and Early Abortion as Risk Factors for Breast Cancer in Young Women," British Journal of Cancer 43:72 (1981).

23. Karen Malec, "Epidemiologic Evidence of an Abortion/Breast Cancer Link" 43 *Journal of American Physicians and Surgeons* vol. 8, no. 2 (Summer 2003).

24. J. R. Maling, "Risk of Breast Cancer Among Young Women Relationship to Induced Abortion," *Journal of the National Cancer Institute* (November 2, 1994) vol. 86, no. 21, pp. 1584-1592.

25. http://www.abortionbreastcancer.com/criteria.htm.

26. Frank, et.al., "Induced Abortion Operations and Their Early Sequelae," *Journal of the Royal College of General Practitioners* (April 1985) vol. 35, no. 73, pp. 175-180.

27. Grimes and Cates, "Abortion: Methods and Complications," *Human Reproduction,* 2nd ed., pp. 796-813.

28. http://www.afterabortion.org/complic.html, 2003, p. 1.

29. Grimes and Cates.

30. Dr. David Reardon, *Aborted Women: Silent No More* (Springfield, Ill: Acorn Books, 2002).
31. http://www.afterabortion.org/complic.html, 2003, p. 3.
32. http://www.afterabortion.org/complic.html, 2003, p. 3.
33. http://www.afterabortion.org/complic.html, 2003, p. 3.
34. Burke and Reardon, p. 33.
35. Trudy Johnson, interview by author, May 2003.
36. Johnson interview.
37. Burke and Reardon, pp. 72, 103, 190-200, 203.
38. Kerri-Ann Kiniorski, "The Aftermath of Abortion," *American Feminist* (March 1, 1998), pp. 6-7.
39. Reardon, *Aborted Women.*
40. Elaine Minamide, "Taboo Grief: Men and Abortion," *Focus on the Family Magazine*, (January 2000), pp. 18-20.
41. Dr. John and Barbara Wilke, *Love Them Both* (Cincinnati, Ohio: Hayes Publishing, 2003), p. 59.
42. Jim Pye, interview by author.
43. Minamide.
44. Burke and Reardon, p. 223.
45. Peggy Hartshorn, interview by author, July 2003.
46. A portion of these questions were suggested by Dr. Burke.

CHAPTER FIVE

1. Anne Pierson, interview by author, July 9, 2003.
2. Kathy Baer, interview by author, May 20, 2003.
3. James L. Gritter, *LifeGivers: Framing the Birthparent Experience in Open Adoption* (Washington, D.C.: Child Welfare League of America), p. 19. Reprinted by permission. http://www.cwla.org.
4. Gritter, pp. 19-22.
5. http://www.christianadoption.com.
6. Naomi Ewald-Orme, interview by author, July 2003.
7. Gritter, p. 33.
8. Baer interview.

CHAPTER SIX

1. Dr. H. Norman Wright, *Loving a Prodigal* (Colorado Springs: Chariot Victor, 1999), p. 103.
2. Karen O'Connor, *Restoring Relationships with Your Adult Children* (Nashville: Thomas Nelson, 1993), p. 98.
3. Julie Parton, interview by author, July 2003.
4. Trica Goyer, interview by author, July 2003.
5. Jeanne Warren Lindsey, interview by author, June 2003.
6. Parton interview.

7. Linda Roggow and Carolyn Owens, *Handbook for Pregnant Teenagers* (Grand Rapids, Mich.: Zondervan, 1984), p. 66.

8. Jeanne Warren Lindsey, *School-Age Parents: The Challenge of Three-Generational Living* (Buena Park: Calif., Morning Glory Press, 1990), p. 144.

9. This list, in part, was adapted from H. Norman Wright, *Surviving a Prodigal: Studies for Parents of Prodigals* (Colorado Springs: David C. Cook, 1999), pp. RS-5C.

CHAPTER SEVEN

1. Sue Powell, interview by author, June 2003.

2. Deborah Brown and Sylvie De Toledo, *Grandparents as Parents: A Survival Guide for Raising a Second Family* (New York: The Guilford Press, 1995), p. 146.

3. Deborah Fuller, RN, MA, MS, interview by author.

4. Karen Peterson, "Grandparents' Labor of Love: Raising Grandkids Is a Tough Job, but Duty Leaves Little Choice," *USA TODAY,* August 6, 2001, pp. 1D-2D.

5. Peterson, pp. 1D-2D.

6. Peterson, pp. 1D-2D.

7. Peterson, pp. 1D-2D.

8. Dr. Lenora M. Poe, "The Changing Family: Social and Emotional Needs of Grandparents Parenting a Second Shift," *GIC Newsletter (the AARP Grandparent Information Center Newsletter),* http://www.aarp.org/grandparents/gpsocialemo.html

9. Betsy Keefer and Jayne Schooler, *Telling the Truth to Your Adopted or Foster Child* (West Port, Conn.: Begin and Garvey, 2000), p. 158.

10. Fuller interview.

11. Fuller interview.

CHAPTER EIGHT

1. Theresa Burke and David Reardon, *Forbidden Grief: The Unspoken Pain of Abortion* (Springfield, Ill.: Acorn Books, 2002), pp. 24-28. (This story is adapted from this resource.)

2. Burke and Reardon, story adaptation.

3. Burke and Reardon, *Forbidden Grief,* p. 28.

4. Dr. David Reardon, "Seven Steps to Healing," accessed at http://afterabortion.info/stepheal.html. Used by permission.

5. http://www.rachelsvineyard.org. Used by permission.

6. http://www.afterabortion.org/stepheal.html.

7. Burke and Reardon, *Forbidden Grief,* pp. 85-86.

8. Burke and Reardon, *Forbidden Grief,* p. 85.

9. Burke and Reardon, *Forbidden Grief,* p. 86.

10. Burke and Reardon, *Forbidden Grief,* p. 92.

11. Dr. Wayne Brauning, "Men and Abortion, Grief and Healing," *Post-Abortion Review,* 4(4) Fall 1996. Dr. Brauning is the founder of Men's Abortion Recovery (MARC). Additional resources covering this subject are available by

writing Dr. Brauning at 237 S. 13th Avenue, Coatsville, PA 19320, or by calling (610) 384-3210.

12. Reardon, "Seven Steps to Healing."
13. Vicki Thorn, interview by author, August 30, 2003.
14. Reardon, "Seven Steps to Healing."
15. David C. Reardon, *The Jericho Plan: Breaking Down the Walls Which Prevent Post-Abortion Healing* (Springfield, Ill: Acorn Books, 1996), p. 27.
16. Adapted from the pamphlet *Your Daughter's Abortion and You* (Colorado Springs: Focus on the Family, 2002).
17. Reardon, "Seven Steps to Healing."
18. Thorn interview.
19. National Office of Post-Abortion Reconciliation and Healing, http://www.noparh.org.
20. Some of these questions were adapted from Linda Cochrane and Kathy Jones, *Healing the Father's Heart: A Post-Abortion Study Guide* (Grand Rapids, Mich.: Baker House, 1996), pp. 17-18.

CHAPTER NINE

1. Betsy Keefer and Jayne Schooler, *Telling the Truth to Your Adopted or Foster Child* (West Port, Conn.: Begin and Garvey, 2000), p. 3.
2. Keefer and Schooler, p. 4.
3. Keefer and Schooler, p. 4.
4. Keefer and Schooler, p. 4.
5. Michael Mask and Julie L. Mask, *Family Secrets* (Nashville: Thomas Nelson, 1995), pp. 9-11.
6. M. Weinrob and B.C. Murphy, "The Birth Mother: A Feminist Perspective for the Helping Professional," *Woman and Therapy* 7, no. 1 (1988), p. 30.
7. These principles were adapted from *Telling the Truth to Your Adopted or Foster Child.* Used with permission.
8. Randolph Severson, *Talking to Your Adopted Adolescent About Adoption: A Collection of the Best Articles on Talking with Kids About Adoption* (San Francisco: PACT Press, 1998).
9. Holly Van Gulden, *Talking with Children About Difficult Birth History: A Collection of the Best Articles on Talking with Kids About Adoption* (San Francisco: PACT Press, 1998).
10. Beth Hall, *Grief: A Collection of the Best Articles on Talking with Kids About Adoption* (San Francisco: PACT Press, 1998).

CHAPTER TEN

1. Adapted from Max Lucado, *In the Eye of the Storm* (Dallas, Tex.: Word, 1991), pp. 144-147.
2. Dr. Jim Fay, taken from *Love and Logic Video Series* (Golden, Col.: Love and Logic Press, 2000).

about the author

FOR MORE THAN twenty years, Jayne Schooler has been using her expertise as an educator, writer, and speaker to do what she loves to do: support, educate, and encourage families formed by adoption or foster care. As a pastor's wife and a parent by both birth and adoption, she brings insight and empathy as she relates warmly to her audiences.

A former adoption coordinator for a public children's services agency in Ohio, Jayne now works full-time as a writer and conference/workshop speaker. She has authored four other books in the field of foster care, adoption, and family life, and contributed over two hundred articles to national and regional publications. She has been a key participant in the development of adoption and foster-care training curriculum for parents and professionals that is used across the country. She regularly conducts workshops on foster/adoptive parent and family life issues on the state and national level for both families and professionals. In recent years, Jayne has been a guest on more than three dozen radio talk shows across the country, speaking on adoption and family life issues.

In addition to training and writing, Jayne shares in the pastoral ministry with her husband, David. She also serves as a faculty member in the Life Issues Counseling Department of the Master's Graduate School of Divinity in Evansville, Indiana. Jayne and her husband are the parents of two adult children: Ray, thirty-seven, who joined their family by adoption at age sixteen, and Kristy, twenty-seven. They have five grandchildren and live in Dayton, Ohio.

UNPLANNED CIRCUMSTANCES, UNEXPECTED GRACE.

The Whole Life Adoption Book

If you're thinking about adopting or have already adopted, Jayne E. Schooler offers encouragement and practical information to help you succeed as an adoptive family.

Jayne E. Schooler
0891097228

God is Good

Make sense of life's pain and tragedy, find fresh hope, and experience the life-changing power of God's love and faithfulness.

Tony Becket
1576833402

To order copies, visit your local Christian bookstore,
call NavPress at 1-800-366-7788,
or log on to www.navpress.com.

To locate a Christian bookstore near you,
call 1-800-991-7747.